DEEP THINKING
IN THE
AGE OF A.I.

WHY CRITICAL THINKING AND DEEP FOCUS
ARE ESSENTIAL IN A MACHINE-DRIVEN WORLD

DONOVAN GARETT

AlgoRhythms Studios, Ltd.

P.O. BOX 35643

Cleveland, Ohio 44135

United States of America

DISCLAIMER. This publication is intended (but not guaranteed) to provide accurate information in regard to the subject matter covered. Some information may not be applicable to every reader or every situation. It is sold with the understanding that neither the author, publisher, nor any other person or entity connected with the creation, publication, or distribution of this publication provides legal, accounting, real estate, or other professional services. If expert assistance is required, the services of a competent professional should be sought.

PRINT ISBN: 978-1-963267-20-4

E-BOOK ISBN: 978-1-963267-21-1

AUDIOBOOK ISBN: 978-1-963267-22-8

Library of Congress Number: 2024918449

Printed in the United States of America

Contents

Chapter 1

The Paradox of Progress

"We marveled at our own magnificence
as we gave birth to AI..."
— Morpheus, "The Matrix" (1999)

I 'M OLD ENOUGH TO remember a time when technology's sole purpose was to serve the needs of humanity. Now, that I'm older, I'm starting to think that, with the dawn of AI, the roles of humanity and technology are shifting. As humans, we are now starting to serve technology.

Let me illustrate . . .

In the 1980s and 1990s, computing relied on the standard operating model of humans inputting data in some form, with the machine manipulating the input based on a predefined algorithm and then generating output used by the human.

Today, however, the model has changed drastically. Humans generate data, which is fed into AI-based algorithms along with the data of thousands (or millions) of others. The AI engine then uses the input data to generate an output that the human uses.

But that's just the beginning . . .

Both the input data and the output data are then fed back into the AI algorithm to make it smarter, along with the collective input and output of millions of others. The machine is learning at an unprecedented rate how humans think and what they need to survive and support each other.

In a very real sense, we are feeding the very machines that are making us obsolete.

And where, exactly, does this data come from? . . .

Everywhere.

Our phones, personal assistants like *Siri* and *Alexa*, the companies we buy from online, our locations, our cars, our movie choices, and on and on.

I wanted to write this book because it's time for us to stop focusing on what AI **can** do, and focus instead on what it **cannot** do (yet) — think on the same level as a human. As humans, we are uniquely designed to think creatively and operate with purpose. However, this requires us to take a step back from technology and focus on developing the very skills that make us uniquely human . . . critical thinking and deep focus.

This chapter explores the paradox of progress: while technology promises to simplify life, it also demands that we cultivate deeper thinking and focus. We will examine how AI's rise creates new opportunities and challenges, emphasizing the need for critical thinking and the ability to engage in meaningful, concentrated work.

The 'Paradox of Progress' Explained

Technology offers us convenience and efficiency that were unimaginable a few decades ago. Yet, this apparent ease comes with a paradox: ***as technology handles more routine tasks, the demand for deep thinking and critical analysis grows***. While it is true that technology allows us to do more with less effort, it also erodes our development of cognitive skills.

The idea behind modern technology is to make our lives easier. Automation frees us from repetitive tasks, while instant access to information and services offers unparalleled convenience. From smart devices that manage our daily schedules to algorithms that recommend products and content, technology is continually optimizing the mundane aspects of life.

However, this ease brings with it a seductive illusion, masking a deeper issue: the diminishing need for problem-solving and critical thinking in everyday situations. When machines handle the details, we often stop engaging in activities that challenge our minds, resulting in a steep decline in our ability to think critically and independently.

The Erosion of Mental Resilience

Overreliance on technology affects more than our ability to think critically; it also erodes our mental resilience. As we become accustomed to constant connectivity and instant gratification, our cognitive abilities suffer. Attention spans shorten, memory weakens, and the capacity for sustained concentration diminishes.

Social media and other digital platforms worsen the problem by encouraging superficial engagement, drawing us away from activities that require deep focus and thoughtful reflection. This shift towards shallow interaction and consumption breeds complacency, where dependence on technology weakens the mental faculties that enable complex thinking and creative problem-solving.

The Paradox Revealed

Despite technology's conveniences, the need for deep thinking and critical analysis has never been more vital. As AI and automation manage an increasing number of routine tasks, the human role must increasingly shift toward solving complex situations where machines lack the nuance and contextual understanding required for effective decision-making.

In this AI-driven world, deep thinking is essential for solving intricate problems, ensuring ethical considerations, and maintaining control over technological systems. Developing deep focus and honing critical thinking skills are vital competitive advantages that allow people to thrive in a world where machines excel at routine tasks. Still, humans must lead in innovation and oversight.

What This Book is About

This book aims to highlight the growing importance of developing and maintaining critical thinking skills in an AI-driven economy. As technology advances, the ability to analyze information, evaluate situations, and make informed decisions will remain a significant competitive advantage.

Additionally, we will explore the concept of deep focus—sustained, uninterrupted concentration on cognitively demanding tasks—and its role in achieving long-term success. By enhancing these skills, you can prepare for a future where human abilities complement, rather than compete with, artificial intelligence.

Books like this are needed because of the current state of distraction that permeates our modern world. With technology now offering constant connectivity and endless entertainment, a growing reliance on digital tools is steadily eroding our capacity for deep thought.

At the same time, there is a persistent gap between what AI can accomplish and what humans can achieve. While AI excels at processing data and routine tasks, it lacks the creativity, judgment, and ethical reasoning that only humans can provide. Bridging this gap requires a renewed commitment to deep thinking and the ability to concentrate intensely, making these skills more critical now than ever.

The strategies outlined in the chapters that follow are designed to help you stay relevant and competitive, whether navigating the modern workplace or focusing on personal development. This book will provide you with a roadmap for thriving amidst continual technological advancements and achieving meaningful success. By using these fundamental skills, you will be better positioned to adapt to and flourish in a rapidly changing work climate.

Let's begin our journey.

Chapter 2
AI's Double-Edged Sword

"Success in creating AI would be the biggest event in human history. Unfortunately, it might also be the last, unless we learn how to avoid the risks."

— Stephen Hawking

───────◄O►───────

ARTIFICIAL INTELLIGENCE AND AUTOMATION are no longer concepts confined to the realms of science fiction; they are integral to our everyday lives. From the way businesses operate to the services we rely on daily, AI and automation have become the central forces driving change across industries.

This chapter explores AI's transformative impact, examining how it is redefining processes, enhancing efficiency, and creating new opportunities. However, with these advancements come challenges, including job displacement and ethical concerns, which require careful consideration.

The Evolution of AI

Artificial intelligence has made significant strides in recent years. Today, AI is characterized by the widespread adoption of machine learning and deep learning algorithms, which have revolutionized AI systems' capabilities and expanded their applications across various domains.

The shift from symbolic AI, which relied on explicit rules and logic, to a dynamic, data-driven approach marked a turning point in the evolution of artificial intelligence. Machine learning, particularly deep learning, has transformed the field by enabling AI systems to learn from vast amounts of data and improve their performance over time.

This transition has led to significant advancements in AI capabilities, such as speech recognition, image processing, and natural language processing. Machines now perform tasks that were once considered the exclusive domain of humans. Deep learning, in particular, has enabled AI to analyze complex patterns and make predictions with remarkable accuracy, driving innovation in areas ranging from healthcare to finance.

Where We're At . . .

Today, AI operates behind the scenes in ways we may not even realize. Virtual assistants like Siri and Alexa use natural language processing to understand and respond to our commands. At the same time, AI-based recommendation systems on platforms like Netflix and Amazon analyze our viewing and shopping behavior to suggest content and products. AI-enhanced social media algorithms curate content to maximize our engagement. Autonomous vehicles leverage AI to traverse city streets, showcasing the technology's potential to disrupt transportation.

The rapid advancement of AI technologies brings a host of ethical dilemmas and challenges. One primary concern is the potential for bias in AI algorithms, arising from flawed training data or design processes, leading to unfair or discriminatory outcomes. Data privacy is another critical issue. AI systems rely on vast amounts of personal data to function effectively, raising questions about how this information is collected, stored, and used.

The potential for AI misuse, whether through malicious applications or unintended consequences, underscores the need for regulatory frameworks and ethical guidelines to ensure that AI development aligns with societal values and promotes the greater good. As AI continues to advance, addressing these ethical challenges will be crucial to harnessing its full potential while mitigating severe risks.

Where We're Going . . .

A key area of focus in AI research is the distinction between narrow AI and general AI. Narrow AI refers to systems designed to perform specific tasks exceptionally well, such as image recognition or language translation, without broader understanding or consciousness.

In contrast, Artificial General Intelligence (or AGI) aims to develop machines that can perform any intellectual task that a human being can, potentially achieving a level of cognition comparable to human intelligence. While narrow AI has seen widespread success and application, AGI remains a theoretical concept, with ongoing debates and research dedicated to exploring its feasibility and the potential impact it could have on society.

The Transformation of the Job Market

Artificial intelligence and automation are not just changing how tasks are performed; they are fundamentally transforming the job market. As AI takes on more roles traditionally filled by people, from routine administrative work to complex analytical tasks, concepts of work and employment are also changing.

Automation, powered by artificial intelligence, is rapidly transforming industries by taking over tasks that humans once performed. This shift is particularly evident in jobs involving repetitive, rule-based activities, which are increasingly being handled by machines designed for efficiency and accuracy.

Robotic Process Automation (RPA) is at the forefront of this transformation, streamlining operations across various sectors. In finance, RPA is used to automate processes like data entry, transaction processing, and compliance checks, reducing errors and freeing up human workers for more strategic tasks.

In manufacturing, robots commonly handle assembly line work, quality control, and inventory management, enhancing productivity and reducing costs. Customer service has also seen significant changes, with AI-powered chatbots and virtual assistants handling common inquiries and routine support tasks.

While automation offers many benefits, it also poses significant challenges for the workforce, particularly for low-skill jobs that are most susceptible to being replaced by machines. Sectors such as manufacturing, retail, and administrative services are experiencing widespread job displacement as automation takes over tasks that humans once performed. This trend is prompting a reevaluation of the types of jobs that will be secure in an AI-dominated future.

The Creation of New Job Categories

While AI and automation are displacing many traditional roles, they are also driving the creation of new job categories. These emerging fields require skills that are not only technical but also interdisciplinary, combining domain expertise with knowledge of AI and machine learning.

As AI continues to advance, there is a growing demand for professionals who can develop, manage, and maintain these technologies. New roles such as data scientists, AI ethics consultants, AI trainers, and AI systems maintainers are becoming increasingly vital.

Data scientists are responsible for designing algorithms and models that enable AI systems to learn and improve, while AI ethics consultants ensure that these technologies are developed and used responsibly, considering the ethical implications, social and societal impact. AI trainers teach machines how to interpret data and make decisions, and AI system maintainers oversee the infrastructure that supports AI operations. These roles require levels of both technical skills and domain knowledge.

The Future Workforce: Skills and Education

Skills must be developed beyond basic technical proficiency to prepare for the future workforce. Critical thinking, creativity, and problem-solving are becoming more important than ever, enabling the next generation of workers to approach complex challenges with innovative solutions.

Education is paramount in equipping the next generation with these skills. Sadly, however, most school curricula today focus on rote memorization and test-passing rather than critical thinking and developing a habit of lifelong learning. In many communities, schools have become veritable *"rescue centers"* — tasked with providing students basic necessities like food, clothing, crisis intervention, and other services once handled by extended family, community, and government programs.

This lack of focus on education has taken a heavy toll on educators and budgets, with little left for teaching the skills necessary to thrive in a technology-based economy. Furthermore, the lack of discipline within school systems has caused many teachers to quit *en masse*, applying their skills to other fields such as finance and technology — further limiting options for students to receive a quality education.

Why Critical Thinking and Focus Matter

As AI continues to reshape the job market, the ability to think critically and maintain deep focus is crucial. Deep thinking allows us to interpret data and understand the broader implications of AI-driven decisions and the complex ethical challenges that arise. Critical thinking complements AI by providing the human judgment necessary to make nuanced decisions that machines cannot. This combination of skills ensures that humans remain essential in guiding AI development and application, maintaining a competitive edge in the workforce.

Lifelong Learning as a Survival Strategy

The rapid pace of technological change means that continuous learning and adaptation are essential for career longevity. Regardless of occupation, a renewed focus on lifelong learning will enable you to stay up-to-date within your chosen field, ensuring you have the skills to succeed in a constantly evolving job market.

The global economy and traditional notions of employment are undergoing significant change in this new era of artificial intelligence. While new opportunities are emerging, some jobs are being rendered entirely obsolete, requiring a shift in how we think about work and the skills necessary to thrive.

To illustrate, let's take a look at the 2023 UAW strike.

Case Study: The 2023 UAW Strike

In 2023, the UAW (United Auto Workers) strike erupted as thousands of autoworkers across the United States walked off the job. The UAW's demands included a 20% immediate raise, a 46% hourly pay increase over time, pension and retiree health care restoration, a four-day workweek, job protections, and assurances that factory work would continue as automakers transition to electric vehicles.[1]

Despite the strike resulting in 25% pay increases and many other concessions, it ultimately led to an unexpected outcome. By 2024, The "Big Three" automakers (i.e., Ford, General Motors, and Stellantis) responded with mass layoffs to offset the added costs. Since the end of the strike in November 2023, over 20,000

---

1. See, e.g., *"Tapping the Brakes: The Effect of the 2023 United Auto Workers Strike on Economic Activity,"* Federal Reserve, retrieved from https://www.federalreserve.gov/econres/notes/feds-notes/tapping-the-br akes-the-effect-of-the-2023-united-auto-workers-strike-on-economic-acti vity-20240416.html

UAW members at the "Big Three" facilities have been laid off (as of the time of writing this book).[2]

What has not been discussed openly is that faced with ongoing labor disputes and the rising costs of meeting worker demands, companies like the "Big Three" automakers have accelerated their investment in AI and Robotic Process Automation (RPA).[3] This reinforces the harsh reality that traditional labor pressures are becoming increasingly ineffective in the face of advancing technology.

Is The Labor Movement Dying?

As artificial intelligence and Robotic Process Automation (RPA) continue to advance, labor protests like the UAW strike in 2023 are becoming irrelevant. Striking and demanding better terms will continue to accelerate the adoption of AI and automation, ultimately displacing the workers these protests are trying to protect.

Strikes may have been effective when human labor was the only option, but that's no longer the case. Today, technology can

---

2. *"Record UAW Contracts = Record UAW Layoffs,"* Labor Pains, https://laborpains.org/2024/06/06/record-uaw-contracts-record-uaw-layoffs/

3. See, e.g., *"Why Robot? Automation To Increase After UAW Deal Costs The Car Industry,"* Benzinga, retrieved from https://www.nasdaq.com/articles/why-robot-automation-to-increase-after-uaw-deal-costs-the-car-industry

replace many factory and assembly jobs — once the backbone of organized labor movements. With each protest, companies are incentivized to accelerate their automation plans, entirely cutting out the middleman—human workers. This means that jobs aren't just at risk; they are being systematically rendered obsolete by machines that can perform the same tasks faster, cheaper, and without complaint.

Many workers fail to realize that companies are only interested in efficiency and profit, not yielding to labor demands. With AI and RPA, companies have a powerful alternative to human labor. When workers strike for higher wages or job security, companies have a straightforward response: invest in technology that doesn't go on strike, require breaks, or need health benefits.

As a result, the more low-skilled workers push for better pay and conditions through traditional labor protests, the faster businesses move to automate. Sadly, this shift means fewer available jobs in an already shrinking pool and less bargaining power for future workers.

A Change in Public Sentiment

Public sympathy for labor movements like the UAW strike has also diminished in recent years, especially as consumers grow less empathetic to the demands of autoworkers who have historically earned top-tier wages for jobs that require relatively low-skilled labor.

For decades, workers such as those in the automotive industry benefited from powerful labor unions that secured substantial pay and benefits packages for roles that did not demand extensive education or specialized skills. This allowed workers to enjoy a standard of living that most other low-skilled workers simply could not achieve.

However, this dynamic is shifting, and public perception is changing along with it. As the cost of new cars has skyrocketed, consumers are looking for cheaper alternatives and are unwilling to pay more to subsidize higher wages for autoworkers.

As many people face their own financial hardships, including stagnant wages and job insecurity, the sight of autoworkers striking for higher pay seems grossly out of touch with the current economic reality. This reflects a broad shift in attitudes about work as technology redefines the value placed on human labor.

Rather than cling to a vanishing work model, the focus must shift to developing skills that machines can't easily replicate. Without change, some workers will become increasingly left behind as AI and automation take over more roles. The bottom line is clear: traditional labor protests are becoming a thing of the past. In an AI-driven world, workers are losing the fight for job security.

The Need for Human Judgment

Amid AI's rise, the value of human judgment, insight, and creativity remains irreplaceable. While AI excels at data processing and predefined algorithms, it lacks the capacity for ethical reasoning, empathy, and nuanced decision-making inherent to humans.

As we will explore in later chapters, many decisions and tasks require a level of understanding and ethical consideration that AI cannot match. Human judgment is critical when empathy, moral principles, and contextual awareness are needed. Balancing AI-driven efficiency with human oversight is vital to ensure that technological progress aligns with societal values and ethical standards. Keeping this delicate balance prevents over-reliance on machines and safeguards the human element in decision-making processes.

In the next chapter, we'll discuss why modern distractions make critical thinking and deep focus so challenging.

Chapter 3
The Dilemma of Distraction

"The so-called modern conveniences may, in fact, be extremely inconvenient - everything seems to exist as a distraction from any sort of deeper thought or contemplation."

— Michael Finkel

———————◄O►———————

OUR ABILITY TO MAINTAIN attention and focus is under unprecedented strain in a world saturated with digital devices and constant connectivity. As devices offer endless streams of information and entertainment at our fingertips, the capacity for deep concentration and sustained thought is diminishing.

In this chapter, we'll take a closer look at how the use of technology is eroding our attention spans and weakening our ability to engage in deep, meaningful work. We will examine the impact of digital distractions on cognitive function, highlighting how modern environments promote superficial engagement and instant gratification.

Understanding the factors contributing to this erosion of focus is crucial, especially as we navigate a world increasingly shaped by artificial intelligence and automation. To thrive in this new landscape, we must reclaim our ability to concentrate deeply and think critically, skills that are more valuable now than ever before.

The Erosion of Attention and Focus

Today, our smartphones, tablets, and computers continually demand our attention with constant notifications, alerts, and updates. Social media platforms, streaming services, and online news are designed to capture and keep our focus, often pulling us away from deeper, more meaningful activities.

The impact of these digital distractions is far-reaching, affecting our cognitive abilities and overall productivity. As our attention becomes more fragmented, our capacity for complex problem-solving and creative thinking declines.

The surge in digital technologies has also profoundly changed how we interact with the world and each other. While these innovations offer convenience and connectivity, they also disrupt our ability to focus.

Smartphones, tablets, and computers are now integral to our daily routines, shaping how we communicate, work, and entertain ourselves. The constant availability of digital content—from news updates to social media feeds—contributes to fragmented attention, making it difficult to engage in sustained concentration.

As our screens increasingly dominate our environment, our capacity for deep, uninterrupted thought is steadily deteriorating, replaced by habits of constantly shifting focus from one digital stimulus to another.

Social Media, Video Games and Streaming Services

Social media platforms are explicitly designed to capture and hold our attention. With features like infinite scrolling, targeted content, and instant notifications, these platforms create dopamine loops that keep users constantly engaged. The pursuit of likes, shares, and comments creates an addictive cycle. Users constantly seek validation and interaction, further distracting them from more productive activities. Over time, this reduces our ability to focus on tasks that require deep cognitive effort.

Video games and streaming services add another layer of digital distraction. The immersive nature of video games draws players into elaborately crafted virtual worlds, offering engagement and escapism that can consume hours at a time.

Similarly, the culture of binge-watching promoted by streaming services encourages prolonged viewing sessions, diminishing attention spans and the ability to engage in more productive activities. Both forms of entertainment provide immediate gratification, making it difficult for individuals to prioritize tasks that require sustained attention and effort.

The Decline of Deep Work

Because of these digital distractions, the practice of deep work—engaging in focused, uninterrupted tasks that require significant cognitive effort—is increasingly rare. The modern work environment, coupled with the constant use of technology, has encouraged a culture where multitasking and constant interruptions are the norms rather than the exceptions. This shift away from deep work has profound implications for our productivity, cognitive function, and overall well-being.

Shifting from Focused to Fragmented Work

The concept of multitasking has long been romanticized in today's work culture and is often seen as a valuable skill. However, research shows that multitasking is not nearly as effective as it seems. Studies have found that when people switch tasks frequently, their productivity drops significantly. One study by the *American Psychological Association* revealed that task-switching can reduce productivity by up to 40% due to the cognitive costs associated with shifting gears between tasks.[1] This constant switching affects the quantity and quality of work performed, as individuals are less likely to engage deeply with any single task.

The modern workplace is rife with distractions, from emails and instant messages to meetings, notifications, and ad-hoc discussions with coworkers. These interruptions create an environment where sustained concentration is very difficult to maintain, pushing employees towards a more fragmented approach to their tasks.

According to a study published in the *Journal of Experimental Psychology: Human Perception and Performance*, even brief interruptions can double the number of errors made by workers, showing the detrimental impact of distractions on accuracy and effectiveness.[2]

This fragmented way of working leads to a superficial engagement with tasks, where the focus is on completing multiple activities rather than excelling in any one.

The Consequences of a Distracted Mind

The cognitive costs of a distracted mind are far-reaching. Distractions and interruptions can impair memory retention, as our brains struggle to encode and store information effectively when constantly interrupted.

A study from the *University of California, Irvine*, found that it takes an average of 23 minutes and 15 seconds to return to a task after being interrupted, highlighting how distractions can severely disrupt workflow and cognitive continuity.[3] This disruption hampers our ability to think deeply and critically, reducing our capacity to solve complex problems and innovate.

Additionally, chronic distraction can lead to a phenomenon known as *"shallow thinking,"* where individuals skim through information without fully processing or understanding it. This type of thinking is amplified by the rapid consumption of digital content, which emphasizes quick, surface-level engagement rather than in-depth analysis. Over time, this can diminish our ability to engage in deep work, affecting our creativity, learning, and overall cognitive function.

---

3. Mark, G., Gudith, D., & Klocke, U. (2008). "The cost of interrupted work: More speed and stress." *Proceedings of the SIGCHI Conference on Human Factors in Computing Systems*. Retrieved from https://ics.uci.edu/~gmar k/chi08-mark.pdf

The long-term impact of this decline in deep work is concerning. As our ability to focus diminishes, so does our potential for meaningful learning and career progression. Professions that require deep analytical thinking, problem-solving, and creativity are particularly at risk, as a distracted mind undermines these skills.

In a study published in the *Proceedings of the National Academy of Sciences*, researchers found that individuals who frequently multitask and are constantly distracted by digital media have less brain density in areas responsible for cognitive and emotional control.[4] This structural change in the brain underscores the lasting effects of chronic distraction and the importance of promoting an environment conducive to deep, focused work.

The Cultural Acceptance of Distraction

The shift towards a more distracted lifestyle isn't solely due to technological advancements; it's also deeply rooted in cultural changes. Society's growing acceptance of constant busyness and multitasking as norms has contributed significantly to the erosion of attention and focus. This cultural shift has far-reaching implications for how individuals perceive productivity and suc-

---

4. Loh, K. K., & Kanai, R. (2014). "Higher Media Multitasking Activity Is Associated with Smaller Gray-Matter Density in the Anterior Cingulate Cortex." *Proceedings of the National Academy of Sciences*, 111(14), 4891-4896. Retrieved from NIH, National Library of Medicine https://www.ncbi.nlm.nih.gov/pmc/articles/PMC4174517/

cess, often blurring the lines between being ***busy*** and being truly ***productive***.

The Normalization of Busyness vs. Productivity

Today, *"busyness"* has become a status symbol. Being busy is often equated with being important, successful, and in demand. This perception is heavily influenced by *"hustle culture,"* which glorifies constant work and multitasking as pathways to success. The rise of hustle culture has fostered a belief that to achieve more, one must constantly be doing something—whether it's working late hours, juggling multiple projects, or staying plugged in around the clock.

This normalization of busyness behaviors has significant consequences. Research shows that people who constantly multitask or feel pressured to stay busy are often less productive and more stressed than those who prioritize focused, deliberate work.

For instance, according to a study by the *Harvard Business Review,* employees who perceived themselves as busy were more likely to overestimate their productivity and contribution, even when their actual output was lower due to fragmented attention.[5] This misperception can lead to a cycle where individuals

---

5. Harvard Business Review. (2016). "The Busier You Are, the More You Need Quiet Time." Retrieved from https://hbr.org/2017/03/the-busier -you-are-the-more-you-need-quiet-time.

embrace "busyness" without realizing its toll on their performance.

The societal embrace of busyness also impacts mental health. Constantly striving to appear busy can lead to burnout, anxiety, and a sense of inadequacy, particularly when individuals feel they are not meeting the expectations set by *"hustle culture."*

According to a report by the *World Health Organization*, burnout has become a widespread phenomenon in the workplace, characterized by chronic stress and a feeling of exhaustion, often stemming from an unrelenting pace of work and the pressure to be constantly productive.[6] A culture of busyness leaves little room for rest, reflection, or deep, meaningful work, further exacerbating the decline of focus and attention.

The cultural acceptance of busyness often reinforces a distracted lifestyle. When society values busyness over quality of work, people are incentivized to prioritize quantity over depth. This mindset is evident in many workplace environments where managers frequently reward employees for their availability and responsiveness rather than the quality or true business value of their contributions.

---

6. World Health Organization. (2019). "Burn-out an 'occupational phenomenon': International Classification of Diseases." Retrieved from https://www.who.int/news/item/28-05-2019-burn-out-an-occupa tional-phenomenon-international-classification-of-diseases.

According to one study, when peripheral tasks interrupt the execution of primary tasks, users require from 3% to 27% more time to complete the tasks, commit twice the number of errors across tasks, experience from 31% to 106% more annoyance, and experience twice the increase in anxiety than when those same peripheral tasks are presented in between primary tasks.[7]

These findings suggest that employees who frequently interrupt their work to respond to emails or attend meetings might perceive themselves as more valuable to their organizations despite evidence that these interruptions severely diminish their productivity and job satisfaction.

This disconnect between perceived and actual productivity highlights the cultural bias towards "busyness" and its detrimental effects on focus and deep work. By recognizing the cultural factors contributing to the normalization of busyness, we can start to challenge these norms by prioritizing focused, meaningful work over mere activity.

The Science Behind Attention and Focus

It is important to understand the underlying scientific principles that govern how our brains process information. In a world filled with constant stimuli, the ability to concentrate deeply and sustain attention has become increasingly valuable—and rare. Let's explore the neurological and psychological foundations of attention and focus and how our brains function in an era of digital distractions.

The Anatomy of Attention

Attention is a critical cognitive function that allows us to focus on specific stimuli while filtering out irrelevant information. It is essential for learning, memory, and everyday functioning.

The brain's ability to allocate focus is a complex process involving several interconnected regions. The *prefrontal cortex*, responsible for executive functions, plays a key role in directing attention and managing tasks that require cognitive control. The *parietal lobe* is also crucial, as it helps shift attention between different stimuli and maintains focus on a specific task. Together, these brain regions work to ensure that we can concentrate on relevant information and ignore distractions.

There are 3 different types of attention that our brain utilizes depending on the situation:

- ***Sustained Attention.*** This type of attention allows

us to focus on a single task over an extended period, which is essential for activities that require prolonged mental effort, such as studying or working on a complex project.

- **Selective Attention.** This form of attention enables us to concentrate on one particular task or piece of information while ignoring other irrelevant stimuli. It is crucial in environments with multiple distractions, allowing us to prioritize and focus on what is most important.

- **Divided Attention.** Also known as multitasking, divided attention involves splitting focus between multiple tasks. While often perceived as efficient, it can significantly reduce the quality of performance on each task due to the brain's limited capacity for handling multiple streams of information simultaneously.

The Limits of Human Attention

Human attention is finite, and *cognitive load theory* explains the limits of how much information our brains can process at once. According to this theory, the brain has a limited capacity for cognitive resources, which can be overwhelmed when too much information is presented simultaneously. When *cognitive load* exceeds this capacity, it leads to diminished attention, increased errors, and reduced ability to process information deeply.[8]

This limitation is particularly evident in the context of digital media, where the constant influx of new information strains our cognitive resources. Research suggests that the constant use of digital devices and the internet is contributing to an *"attention span crisis,"* reflecting the growing challenge of maintaining focus in a world where digital distractions are everywhere.

Neuroplasticity and Technology's Impact on the Brain

The constant use of digital devices has fundamentally changed how our brains function. While technology offers countless benefits and conveniences, its constant presence is reshaping our neural pathways and affecting our cognitive abilities.

Neuroplasticity is the brain's remarkable ability to reorganize itself by forming new neural connections throughout life. This adaptability allows us to learn new skills, recover from injuries, and adapt to new environments. However, in the digital age, constant exposure to digital stimuli is rewiring our brains to our detriment.

---

8. See, e.g., Sweller, John. "Cognitive load during problem solving: Effects on learning." Retrieved from https://onlinelibrary.wiley.com/doi/abs/10.12 07/s15516709cog1202_4

With the frequent use of smartphones, tablets, and computers, our brains are becoming conditioned to respond to rapid, fragmented bursts of information. This shift promotes shorter attention spans and a preference for instant gratification over sustained focus and deep thinking.

Maryanne Wolf, a renowned scholar of literacy and the brain at *UCLA's School of Education & Information Studies*, stated the following:

> *"The subtle atrophy of critical analysis and empathy affects us all. It affects our ability to navigate a constant bombardment of information," she writes. "It incentivizes a retreat to the most familiar silos of unchecked information, which require and receive no analysis, leaving us susceptible to false information and demagoguery."* [9]

Similar research has found that heavy internet users showed more activity in the prefrontal cortex, the part of the brain associated with decision-making and problem-solving, suggesting that frequent internet use may be training the brain to become

---

9. UCLA School of Education and Information Studies, *"Maryanne Wolf: Skimming While Reading Changes Critical Thinking and Empathy,"* retrieved from https://seis.ucla.edu/news/maryanne-wolf-skimming-while-reading-changes-critical-thinking-and-empathy/

more adept at skimming information rather than engaging in deep processing.

While neuroplasticity enables this adaptation, it also presents a challenge: the more we engage in quick, superficial interactions online, the more our brains become wired to prefer these types of activities. However, neuroplasticity also offers an opportunity for developing focus. By deliberately practicing sustained attention and minimizing distractions, we can train our brains to enhance concentration and cognitive control, counteracting the negative effects of constant digital engagement.

The Effects of Multitasking

Multitasking is often seen as a valuable skill, but the reality is that our brains are simply not designed to focus on multiple tasks simultaneously. When we attempt to multitask, we are not actually doing two things at once; instead, we are rapidly switching our attention between tasks. This process, known as *task-switching*, is cognitively demanding and significantly reduces efficiency and performance.

Research has shown that multitasking can lead to a substantial decline in cognitive performance. For instance, a study from *Stanford University* found that individuals who frequently multitask with digital media perform worse on tasks requiring sustained attention and memory than those who do not multitask as often.[10] The study also revealed that heavy multitaskers are more easily distracted and have more difficulty filtering out irrelevant information, which hampers their ability to focus on important tasks.

Beyond cognitive performance, multitasking can also negatively impact mental health. Constantly switching between tasks increases cognitive load and can lead to feelings of stress and anxiety. A study published in the *Journal of the Association for Consumer Research* found that frequent multitasking is associated with higher levels of perceived stress, lower self-reported life satisfaction, and decreased emotional well-being.[11]

The strain of juggling multiple tasks can often leave us feeling overwhelmed and mentally exhausted, highlighting the detrimental effects of multitasking on both cognitive function and mental health.

The Attention Economy

In the digital age, attention has become one of the most valuable commodities. Tech companies compete fiercely for user attention, designing products and platforms to capture and hold focus for as long as possible. This competition has given rise to what is known as the *"attention economy,"* where the primary currency is not money, but the time and focus of users.

The Business of Capturing Attention

Large tech companies have perfected the art of capturing user attention. From social media platforms to streaming services, these products are purposely designed to be as engaging as possible, employing various psychological techniques to keep users hooked.

For example, the infinite scroll feature, common on platforms like Facebook and Twitter, ensures that there is no natural stopping point, encouraging users to continue browsing indefinitely. Similarly, push notifications and alerts are strategically timed to draw users back into the app whenever they might otherwise disengage.

The economics of attention explains why capturing user focus is so valuable. In the attention economy, the more time users spend on a platform, the more data they generate. This data can then be used to target ads more effectively, increasing revenue for the company.

As a result, tech companies have a vested interest in keeping users engaged for as long as possible. A study by the *Pew Research Center* found that over 70% of American adults now use social media regularly, indicating just how successful these strategies have been in monopolizing user attention.[12]

The Battle for Focus

To dominate the attention economy, tech companies employ sophisticated strategies to maximize user engagement. Algorithms play a crucial role in this process, analyzing user behavior to deliver personalized content that will most likely resonate with them.

This personalization creates a feedback loop in which users are continually exposed to content that aligns with their preferences and behaviors, making it even harder to disengage. Features like infinite scrolling, which eliminates natural stopping points, and autoplay, which automatically starts the next video, further ensure that users remain on the platform longer than they might have intended.

However, the relentless battle for focus has significant psychological impacts. Constant engagement with digital platforms can lead to anxiety and F.O.M.O. (fear of missing out) as users feel pressured to stay updated and connected at all times. A

---

12. Pew Research Center. (2021). "Social Media Fact Sheet." Retrieved from https://www.pewresearch.org/internet/fact-sheet/social-media/

study published in the *Journal of Social and Clinical Psychology* found that reducing social media use to just 30 minutes per day resulted in significant reductions in anxiety, depression, and feelings of loneliness.[13]

Additionally, the constant barrage of information and choices can lead to decision fatigue, where the quality of decisions deteriorates after an extended decision-making period. This can further result in decreased productivity and mental exhaustion, underscoring the significant toll that the attention economy can take on mental health.

By understanding the mechanics of the attention economy and the psychological effects of constant engagement, we can make more informed choices about how we interact with digital platforms, protecting our focus and mental well-being.

In the next chapter, we'll broaden our scope a bit and look at the consequences of divided attention on our society as a whole. We'll also explore some tips for reclaiming focus.

---

13. Hunt, M. G., Marx, R., Lipson, C., & Young, J. (2018). "No More FOMO: Limiting Social Media Decreases Loneliness and Depression." *Journal of Social and Clinical Psychology*, 37(10), 751-768. Retrieved from https://guilfordjournals.com/doi/10.1521/jscp.2018.37.10.751

Chapter 4

The Consequences of a Distracted Society

"Everybody gets so much information all day long that they lose their common sense."

— Gertrude Stein

———◆○◆———

A S OUR WORLD BECOMES increasingly dominated by digital technology, the effects of widespread distraction are more evident. A society that is constantly diverted by digital stimuli faces significant consequences that go beyond individual productivity or focus.

In this chapter, we'll examine some of the broader implications of living in a distracted society, from deteriorating mental health to declining social cohesion. We'll also discuss practical tips for reclaiming focus in a distracted world.

The Decline in Critical Thinking Skills

Across all ages, cultures, backgrounds, and ethnicities, critical thinking skills are declining rapidly. The constant barrage of information that encourages shallow, surface-level processing is undermining the ability to engage in deep, analytical thought. This shift in cognitive habits has far-reaching implications, especially in the pursuit of education, where the capacity to focus deeply and think critically is essential.

Shallow Thinking vs. Deep Thinking

Constant distraction from digital media leads to shallow thinking, where information is processed quickly and superficially without really engaging in deeper analysis or reflection. This kind of thinking prioritizes superficial understanding and quick decision-making over a thorough exploration of ideas and concepts. As a result, individuals are more likely to rely on snap judgments and simplistic interpretations rather than considering all aspects of a complex situation or problem.

Research has proven that the more we are distracted, the more our ability to think deeply and critically deteriorates. A study conducted by the *University of London* and quoted by *Forbes* magazine found that frequent interruptions and multitasking can reduce cognitive performance to the level of someone who has been smoking marijuana or has lost a night of sleep.[1]

This shallow engagement with information results in a decline in analytical thinking, where the preference for fast, easy-to-digest content overtakes the desire for in-depth understanding and contemplation. This shift can have serious consequences, as it limits the ability to solve complex problems and make informed decisions based on a comprehensive evaluation of all relevant factors.

The Impact on Education and Knowledge

The decline in critical thinking is particularly concerning in education, where deep learning and understanding are paramount. Both educators and students are struggling to adapt to a learning environment increasingly impacted by digital distractions.

Teachers find it challenging to maintain student engagement when competing against the allure of smartphones and social media, which offer immediate gratification and constant entertainment. Meanwhile, students find it harder to concentrate for extended periods, resulting in a shallow grasp of subjects requiring sustained attention and thought.

---

1. Forbes. "Why Multi-Tasking Is Worse Than Marijuana For Your IQ." Retrieved from https://www.forbes.com/sites/vanessaloder/2014/06/11/why-multi-tasking-is-worse-than-marijuana-for-your-iq/

The shift from deep reading habits to quick consumption of snippets and sound bites further exacerbates the problem. The practice of deep reading, which involves immersing oneself in a text and engaging critically with its content, is being replaced by skimming and scanning short, easily digestible pieces of information. This trend is evident in the decline of book reading and the rise of online content that is often designed for quick consumption.

According to a report by the *Pew Research Center*, roughly a quarter (23%) of American adults did not read a single book in any format in 2021.[2] As people move away from reading, they lose opportunities to develop critical thinking skills and are more likely to struggle with understanding complex ideas and nuanced arguments.

Professional and Personal Consequences

The consequences of a distracted society extend beyond cognitive skills and education, significantly affecting both professional and personal spheres. In the workplace, the constant barrage of distractions leads to decreased productivity and lower job satisfaction, while in personal life, it weakens relationships and impairs the ability to maintain meaningful connections.

---

2. Pew Research Center. (2021). "Who Doesn't Read Books in America?" Retrieved from https://www.pewresearch.org/short-reads/2021/09/21/who-doesnt-read-books-in-america/

Decreased Productivity and Job Satisfaction

Distractions in the workplace have become a major contributor to decreased productivity and job dissatisfaction. With the prevalence of digital notifications, emails, and the temptation to browse social media, employees find it increasingly difficult to maintain focus on their assigned tasks.

This constant switching of attention between tasks leads to what is known as *"task-switching cost,"* which significantly reduces efficiency and increases the likelihood of errors. A study by the *University of California, Irvine*, found that after only 20 minutes of interrupted performance, people reported significantly higher stress, frustration, workload, effort, and pressure.[3]

The effects of distraction also contribute to rising levels of burnout and stress. As employees struggle to keep up with the demands of their jobs amidst a sea of interruptions, they often experience a sense of overwhelm and frustration. According to a report by *Gallup*, 76% of employees experience burnout, with distractions and workload management being key contrib-

---

3. Mark, G., Gudith, D., & Klocke, U. (2008). "The cost of interrupted work: More speed and stress." *Proceedings of the SIGCHI Conference on Human Factors in Computing Systems.* Retrieved from https://ics.uci.edu/~gmark/chi08-mark.pdf

utors.[4] This environment reduces job satisfaction and hampers career growth, as constant distractions lead to lost time and decreased performance, ultimately impacting long-term professional development.

The Effect on Personal Relationships

Distractions are not just a professional issue; they also take a significant toll on personal relationships. One significant way is through *"phubbing,"* or phone snubbing, where individuals prioritize their phones over the people they are with. Phubbing has been shown to negatively affect relationship satisfaction and create feelings of neglect and resentment. A study published in the *Journal of Social and Personal Relationships* associated phubbing behaviors with decreased relationship satisfaction and increased conflict.[5]

As digital devices constantly vie for our attention, maintaining meaningful conversations and relationships becomes increasingly challenging. The presence of smartphones and other devices can hinder deep, focused conversations, reducing the qual-

---

4. Gallup. (2020). "Employee Burnout: Causes and Cures." Retrieved from https://www.gallup.com/workplace/288539/employee-burnout-causes-cures.aspx

5. Roberts, J. A., & David, M. E. (2016). "My life has become a major distraction from my cell phone: Partner phubbing and relationship satisfaction among romantic partners." *Computers in Human Behavior*, 54, 134-141. Retrieved from https://psycnet.apa.org/record/2015-49557-016

ity of our interactions. Research from the *University of Essex* demonstrated that the mere presence of a mobile phone during a conversation can lower the quality of that interaction, leading to less empathy and connection between individuals.[6] This ongoing distraction in personal interactions makes it challenging to form and maintain significant relationships.

The Societal Implications

The consequences of living in a distracted society extend far beyond individual productivity and personal relationships. At a societal level, the prevalence of distractions and the constant bombardment of information are reshaping how we process information, engage in public discourse, and make collective decisions.

The Risk of Information Overload

As we are inundated with information from countless sources, the overwhelming amount of information, often called *"information overload,"* can lead to confusion, misinformation, and decision paralysis. Excessive information makes it challenging to discern what is accurate, relevant, and trustworthy. This

---

6. Przybylski, A. K., & Weinstein, N. (2013). "Can you connect with me now? How the presence of mobile communication technology influences face-to-face conversation quality." *Journal of Social and Personal Relationships*, 30(3), 278-286. Retrieved from https://journals.sagepub.com/doi/10.1177/0265407512453827.

confusion often creates an environment where misinformation thrives as we struggle to filter out unreliable sources from credible ones.

The issue of information overload also contributes to a decline in public discourse. Where superficial engagement replaces in-depth analysis, meaningful debate is undermined. Social media platforms, designed to prioritize speed and virality over accuracy and depth, encourage quick reactions rather than thoughtful consideration.

This shift has led to a rise in *"echo chambers,"* where individuals are exposed primarily to viewpoints that reinforce their own instead of ideas that challenge their assumptions — further polarizing society. The lack of critical engagement with differing perspectives hampers the ability to have informed debates and make collective decisions that are in the best interest of the public.

The Future of a Distracted Society

If the trend of distraction continues unchecked, the potential long-term consequences for society are concerning, to say the least. A distracted society risks losing the capacity for deep thinking, creativity, and practical problem-solving—all essential qualities for addressing complex challenges.

As attention spans shorten and the ability to engage with nuanced ideas diminishes, there is a danger that society will become much more reactive and much less reflective, making it harder for individuals to comprehend and navigate the subtle complexities of life.

Reclaiming Attention and Focus

Reclaiming our ability to focus and maintain attention is more critical than ever. The decline in deep thinking, the erosion of meaningful relationships, and the impact on both personal and professional life underscore the need for a deliberate effort to regain control over our mental faculties.

Acknowledging the problem is the first step toward regaining control over our attention and focus. By becoming aware of the factors contributing to distraction and understanding their costs, we can begin to take meaningful steps toward reclaiming our ability to engage deeply with the world around us.

Beware of Distraction Triggers

To combat distraction, it's important to identify the personal and environmental factors contributing to it. Distraction triggers can vary widely from person to person and may include anything from digital notifications and social media to environmental factors like noisy environments or cluttered workspaces. Understanding these triggers requires a mindful approach, where you consciously observe how, when, where, and why your attention is being diverted.

Mindfulness plays a key role in realizing that attention is being pulled away from more important tasks. By practicing mindfulness, you can develop a heightened awareness of your mental state and identify specific moments when distraction occurs. This allows for greater self-control and the ability to redirect focus back to the task at hand. Over time, becoming more attuned to distraction triggers can help you create environments and routines that support sustained attention and deep work.

Periodic self-reflection is also essential. By evaluating how distractions affect your daily routines, relationships, and long-term goals, you can gain clarity on what changes are needed to improve focus. This process involves honestly assessing the role that digital devices and other distractions play in life and weighing the benefits of reducing or eliminating these influences. Through self-reflection, you will develop a more intentional approach to managing your attention and prioritize activities that align with your values and objectives.

Practical Strategies for Regaining Focus

Once the problem of distraction is recognized, the next step is to implement practical approaches for regaining focus. Over time, these techniques will help you reduce over-reliance on digital devices and cultivate habits that support deep work and sustained attention.

Try a Digital Detox

One effective strategy for regaining focus is a digital detox, which involves taking intentional breaks from technology to restore mental clarity and attention. Unplugging from digital devices, even for short periods, can help reduce mental fatigue and improve concentration. Research suggests that regular breaks from screens can decrease stress levels and enhance overall well-being, making it easier to engage deeply with tasks when returning to work.

Practical steps for reducing digital consumption include setting clear boundaries around technology use, such as limiting screen time in the evenings or designating tech-free zones in the home. Using focus apps that block distracting websites and notifications during work hours can also be beneficial. Additionally, scheduling regular tech-free times, such as a digital detox weekend or a daily unplugged hour, can create space for reflection, relaxation, and reconnection with the physical world.

Building Habits for Deep Work

Cultivating habits that support deep work is essential for maintaining focus in a distraction-heavy environment. Establishing a routine can help create a sense of structure and predictability, making engaging in deep, focused work easier. Creating a dedicated workspace free from distractions, setting specific goals for work sessions, and using time-blocking techniques to allocate periods for focused work all contribute to a more productive and fulfilling work experience.

Techniques for improving focus, such as meditation, mindfulness, and cognitive training exercises, can further boost your ability to concentrate. Meditation and mindfulness practices help train the mind to remain present and attentive, reducing the impact of external distractions. Cognitive training exercises, which challenge the brain to focus on complex tasks or solve puzzles, often improve cognitive flexibility and attention control. By incorporating these practices into your daily routine, you can strengthen your focus and build resilience against the pull of distractions.

In the next chapter, we'll discuss the vital role of critical thinking in the age of AI.

Chapter 5

Why Critical Thinking is Essential in the AI Age

"Learning without thought is labor lost;
thought without learning is perilous."

— Confucius

---◦○◦---

A S ARTIFICIAL INTELLIGENCE BECOMES more integrated into every aspect of our lives, the ability to think critically is emerging as one of the most valuable skills for navigating this new landscape. At a time when machines can perform many tasks faster and more efficiently than humans, our unique capacity for critical thinking—evaluating information, making reasoned decisions, and solving complex problems—sets us apart.

This chapter explores the importance of critical thinking skills, emphasizing how they can empower individuals to thrive in a world increasingly dominated by technology. We will examine how critical thinking helps us make informed decisions amidst the overwhelming influx of information. We will also discuss the role of critical thinking in ensuring ethical AI development and usage and its impact on personal and professional growth.

What is Critical Thinking?

Critical thinking is composed of several components, each playing a crucial role in the process of analyzing and synthesizing information:

- *Analysis.* This is the ability to break down complex information into manageable parts, identifying patterns, relationships, and underlying structures. Analysis helps us understand the facets of an issue or argument and how they interact with one another. By dissecting information, we can better understand the whole picture and make more informed judgments.

- *Evaluation.* Evaluation involves assessing the credibility, relevance, and accuracy of information. This requires a person to determine the validity of sources, identify biases, and assess the strength of arguments and evidence. Through evaluation, we can distinguish between reliable and unreliable information, ensuring that decisions are based on sound evidence.

- *Inference.* Inference is the ability to draw logical conclusions based on available evidence. This involves recognizing implicit assumptions, making predictions, and forming hypotheses. By making inferences, we fill gaps in knowledge and make educated guesses about situations or problems, even when all the facts are not immediately available.

- *Interpretation.* Interpretation involves understanding and explaining the meaning of information. It requires the ability to comprehend data, texts, or situations and explain them clearly and meaningfully. Interpretation is crucial for effective communication and making sense of complex or ambiguous information.

- *Explanation.* Explanation is the ability to articulate the reasoning and thought process behind conclusions. It involves presenting arguments in a coherent and logical manner, supporting them with evidence, and clearly stating the rationale for decisions. Clear explanation helps ensure that others understand our reasoning, encouraging transparency and accountability.

The Importance of Metacognition

Metacognition, or *"thinking about thinking,"* is another essential aspect of critical thinking. It involves self-awareness and self-regulation of our cognitive processes, allowing us to evaluate and adjust our thinking strategies to improve understanding and problem-solving. It involves reflecting on how we think, recognizing our thought patterns, and evaluating the effectiveness of our reasoning. This self-awareness helps us identify cognitive biases and errors, which can severely distort our judgment and decision-making.

Metacognition enhances critical thinking by allowing us to correct preconceptions and errors in our reasoning. When we understand our approach to thinking, we are better equipped to adjust it to fit different situations, leading to more effective problem-solving and decision-making. This self-reflective practice helps us develop a more disciplined and rigorous approach to thinking, facing complex issues with greater clarity and precision.

Why Critical Thinking is Essential in the AI Era

As AI continues to evolve, the importance of critical thinking has never been more evident. While AI excels in processing large amounts of data and performing specific tasks with speed and accuracy, it has significant limitations in areas that require contextual understanding, ethical judgment, and nuanced decision-making.

For instance, an AI algorithm may be able to identify patterns in hiring data and suggest candidates based on quantitative metrics. Still, it might miss the importance of diversity, cultural fit, or ethical considerations in hiring decisions. These limitations highlight why critical thinking and human oversight are needed to ensure AI-driven decisions align with broader human values and ethical standards.

The Increasing Demand for Critical Thinking At Work

As AI continues to automate routine and repetitive tasks, the nature of work is changing. Tasks that once required straightforward decision-making are now handled by machines, freeing up human workers to focus on more complex and creative endeavors. This shift is increasing the demand for critical thinking in the workplace, where human judgment is needed to address ambiguous situations, solve complex problems, and navigate ethical challenges.

Critical thinking plays a pivotal role in AI-driven industries, including decision-making, innovation, and leadership. Leaders and employees must be able to analyze information critically, evaluate the potential impacts of AI-driven decisions, and innovate in ways that leverage both human and machine capabilities.

The ability to think critically enables us to challenge assumptions, consider alternative perspectives, and develop strategies that are not only effective but also ethically sound. As a result, critical thinking is becoming one of the most sought-after skills in the modern workplace, essential for innovation, strategic decision-making, and ensuring responsible AI adoption.

How Critical Thinking Complements AI

As artificial intelligence continues to permeate our lives, we need to understand how it can complement our natural human abilities. AI lacks the capacity for judgment, creativity, and ethical reasoning that are inherently human. This is where critical thinking comes in—providing the nuanced understanding and decision-making capabilities that AI cannot match.

Combining the strengths of human and machine intelligence allows a more balanced approach to problem-solving and decision-making. This not only enhances AI's effectiveness but also ensures that its application aligns with human values and moral considerations.

Human-AI Collaboration

AI systems cannot understand context, exercise ethical judgment, or think creatively. Therefore, human oversight is needed to monitor AI outputs to ensure ethical use and mitigate risks. AI systems can make decisions based on patterns in data, but they do not inherently understand the ethical implications or broader social impact of those decisions.

For instance, in the criminal justice system, AI algorithms are sometimes used to assess defendants' likelihood of recidivism. While these tools can provide valuable insights, they can also perpetuate biases if not carefully monitored. Human judgment ensures that decisions are not solely based on raw data but also consider broader societal implications. By providing this oversight, we can prevent AI from making decisions that may be technically accurate but ethically or morally problematic.

Critical thinking improves AI models by identifying biases, refining algorithms, and interpreting results. Even the most advanced AI systems are only as good as the data they are trained on and the algorithms that guide them. We must use critical thinking skills to scrutinize these elements, uncovering biases that might skew AI's decisions or identifying areas where algorithms may need refinement. This process ensures that AI systems are not just technically proficient but also fair, ethical, and aligned with human values.

Critical Thinking in AI-Driven Decision-Making

As AI becomes more essential to decision-making processes, the ability to critically evaluate AI-generated recommendations is increasingly important. AI outputs are not inherently aligned with human goals or ethical standards. Critical thinking enables us to assess AI-generated decisions, challenge their validity, and ensure they are applied in ways that serve society as a whole.

Critical thinking skills are needed to carefully scrutinize the algorithms used, the quality and representativeness of the data, and the assumptions underlying AI models. This allows humans to assess the strengths and limitations of AI-generated insights and determine their relevance and appropriateness for specific use cases.

Moreover, challenging and validating AI outputs is necessary to ensure they align with societal goals and ethical standards. AI systems can sometimes produce results that, while statistically sound, may not be suitable when considering broader ethical, social, or cultural implications. In these cases, critical thinking is also required to identify potential biases, question the fairness of the recommendations, and consider alternative actions that better align with ethical standards and societal values.

Balancing AI's Efficiency with Human Values

Integrating AI's efficiency with the nuanced, value-driven decisions required in complex scenarios presents another significant challenge. AI cannot appreciate the complexities of human values and moral considerations. Decisions are often made not just based on efficiency or accuracy but also involve weighing competing values, addressing moral dilemmas, and considering long-term impacts on individuals and communities.

Critical thinking is vital in balancing AI efficiency and human values. It allows decision-makers to go beyond the surface-level analysis provided by AI and delve into the deeper implications of AI-driven actions. By applying critical thinking, we can ensure that AI tools are used in ways that serve humanity's best interests, prioritizing not just technical correctness but also fairness, justice, and the well-being of society. This balanced approach is essential for leveraging AI's capabilities while safeguarding the ethical standards and human values that support a just and equitable society.

In the next chapter, we'll discuss practical ways to develop and hone critical thinking skills.

Chapter 6

How To Develop Critical Thinking Skills

"My father used to say, 'Don't raise your voice,
improve your argument."

— Desmond Tutu

———◆O◆———

As AI CONTINUES TO influence our lives, developing strong critical thinking skills is essential for evaluating AI-driven recommendations and ensuring that technology is used ethically and responsibly. By cultivating a mindset of curiosity, skepticism, and reflection, we can better complement AI's capabilities with our unique human strengths.

This chapter will discuss how to develop critical thinking skills. These techniques will help you cultivate a mindset that questions assumptions, evaluates evidence, and thinks strategically.

The Foundations of Critical Thinking

Critical thinking involves analyzing information, evaluating evidence, and reasoning logically to form sound judgments. In the face of rapid technological advancements and the growing influence of artificial intelligence, strong critical thinking skills are crucial. By building a solid foundation in critical thinking, you can enhance your ability to assess situations clearly, make informed choices, and approach problems with greater confidence and creativity.

Components of Critical Thinking

Critical thinking involves systematically analyzing, evaluating, and interpreting information. Mastering these fundamental skills will improve your problem-solving ability.

1. Analysis and Interpretation

At the heart of critical thinking is the ability to **analyze** and **interpret** information. Analysis involves breaking down complex information into more manageable parts, making it easier to understand and evaluate. This helps make sense of data, identify key points, and understand relationships between seemingly dissimilar pieces of information.

Here are some practical exercises to help you build your analytical skills:

- *Case Studies.* Use case studies to practice dissecting real-world situations, spotting the core problems, and weighing different solutions. By learning from past scenarios and their outcomes, you'll gain valuable insights into effective decision-making that you can apply to new challenges.

- *Logic Puzzles.* Challenge yourself with logic puzzles and brainteasers to sharpen your thinking. These exercises encourage you to recognize patterns, draw connections, and solve problems systematically. They're a fun and engaging way to build the mental muscles needed for critical thinking.

- *Scenario Analysis.* Imagine different hypothetical situations and think through their potential outcomes. This helps you anticipate future challenges, evaluate the pros and cons of various decisions, and think strategically about your options. You'll learn to approach problems from various angles and make more thoughtful choices.

- *Deconstruct Complex Information.* When faced with a complex issue, it's essential to deconstruct the information into its fundamental components. This helps in identifying patterns, understanding underlying principles, and pinpoint critical elements that require further scrutiny.

In addition to analyzing information, it is important to know how to interpret the data to draw meaningful conclusions. Effective interpretation goes beyond mere observation; it involves drawing meaning from data and understanding its implications.

One helpful technique is learning to differentiate between *correlation* and *causation*. While correlation indicates a relationship between two variables, causation suggests that one variable directly affects the other. Understanding this distinction is critical to making accurate assessments and avoiding common logic errors.

2. Evaluation and Inference

Another essential component of critical thinking is the ability to *evaluate* information and make *inferences* based on the available evidence. Evaluation involves assessing the credibility and relevance of sources, determining the validity of arguments, and identifying any potential biases.

Remember that not all information is created equal. It's essential to consider sources for reliability and relevance critically. This includes checking credentials, considering the publication date, and recognizing potential biases that might influence the information presented.

Making inferences involves using available evidence to draw conclusions. This requires identifying assumptions that underlie arguments, recognizing biases, and spotting ***logical fallacies***—errors in reasoning that undermine an argument's validity.

3. Explanation and Reflection

The final components of critical thinking involve the ability to ***explain*** your reasoning and engage in meaningful ***reflection***. Explanation requires articulating your thought process clearly and concisely, ensuring that others can understand your reasoning and conclusions.

Explaining your reasoning is vital for communication and collaboration. Whether you're presenting an argument, making a decision, or solving a problem, clear articulation helps ensure that others understand your thought process. This involves sharing your conclusions and explaining the steps you took to arrive at them, the evidence you considered, and how you weighed different factors.

Reflection is another essential part of the critical thinking process. It involves looking back on your decisions, considering alternative perspectives, and evaluating the outcomes of your choices. By reflecting on past experiences, you can identify what worked well, what didn't, and why. This continuous cycle of reflection and learning helps you refine your critical thinking skills.

By mastering these components—analysis, interpretation, evaluation, inference, explanation, and reflection—you can develop a more robust approach to critical thinking. These skills enhance your ability to understand and process information and empower you to make more informed, logical, and thoughtful decisions in both your personal and professional life.

The Role of Curiosity in Critical Thinking

Curiosity is your secret weapon for enhancing critical thinking. It's what drives you to ask questions, dig deeper, and challenge the status quo. Being curious keeps you engaged and open to learning. When you nurture a curious mindset, you're more inclined to explore new ideas, consider different viewpoints, and get to the root of problems—all of which are key to thinking critically.

A curious mindset is characterized by an eagerness to learn and a willingness to explore the unknown. This inquisitive approach is essential for critical thinking, as it encourages ongoing inquiry and helps uncover the underlying truths behind complex issues.

At its core, curiosity is about asking questions and seeking deeper understanding. It pushes a person to go beyond surface-level information and investigate further, uncovering insights that might otherwise remain hidden. By continually questioning the world around us and exploring diverse topics, curiosity helps expand our knowledge base and fosters a more comprehensive understanding of complex subjects.

Here are some practical ways to cultivate curiosity:

- *Ask Better Questions.* Start by shifting your focus from finding quick answers to asking questions that spark deeper thought. Instead of asking, *"What's the answer?"* try asking, *"Why does this happen?"* or *"What if we looked at this differently?"* These questions will lead you to explore further.

- *Challenge Your Assumptions.* Make it a habit to question what you believe and what others present as fact. This helps spot biases and encourages a more thorough understanding. For instance, when you encounter a common belief, ask yourself, *"Why do I believe this?"* and *"Is there another way to look at this?"*

- *Seek Different Perspectives.* Actively seek opportunities to learn from people with different backgrounds and experiences. Considering diverse viewpoints can broaden your thinking and help you approach problems differently. The more perspectives you consider, the stronger your critical thinking skills will become.

By nurturing curiosity, you set yourself up for a more engaging and thoughtful approach to life. Embracing a mindset that values questions over answers generally leads to a deeper probe of subjects and a more nuanced understanding of the world.

Overcoming Barriers to Critical Thinking

Developing strong critical thinking skills isn't just about learning new techniques; it's also about recognizing and overcoming the obstacles that can hinder your ability to think clearly and objectively. Cognitive biases and information overload are two of the most significant barriers to critical thinking.

Cognitive Biases

Cognitive biases are mental shortcuts or tendencies that can skew your thinking and lead to flawed reasoning. These biases are ingrained in modern mass media, such as news coverage, political commentary, and TV commercials. Most people don't even realize they exist. Still, they can prevent you from evaluating information objectively.

Some of the most common cognitive biases include ***confirmation bias***, where you favor information that supports your existing beliefs; the ***availability heuristic***, which causes you to overestimate the importance of information that comes to mind easily; and ***anchoring***, where you rely too heavily on the first piece of information you encounter when making decisions. These biases can subtly influence your thought processes, often without realizing it.

The first step in overcoming cognitive biases is developing ***self-awareness***. Pay attention to your initial reactions to new information and ask yourself whether it is based on objective evaluation or influenced by preconceived notions.

Questioning assumptions is another key strategy; regularly challenge your beliefs and consider alternative viewpoints. Finally, *seeking diverse perspectives* can help you gain a more balanced view and reduce biases. By actively engaging with different ideas and viewpoints, you can broaden your understanding and make more informed judgments.

Information Overload

We are constantly bombarded with information, which can make us feel overwhelmed. This can impede the ability to process information and think critically. Managing this constant influx of data is essential for maintaining focus and clarity in our thinking.

With so much information at our fingertips, it's easy to lose sight of what's important. We often struggle to keep up, jumping from one piece of information to another without understanding (or retaining) any of it. This constant overflow frequently leads to confusion, stress, and a weakened ability to think deeply and critically.

To avoid becoming overwhelmed, *prioritize* the information most relevant to your needs and goals. Learn to focus on what's important and let go of the rest. *Selective filtering* is another helpful technique—use reliable sources and tools to sift through information and identify what's most valuable. Lastly, *focus research* by setting clear objectives and sticking to them. Concentrate on specific questions, issues, or topics and explore them in-depth rather than allowing yourself to be distracted by every new piece of information.

Complacency and Echo Chambers

While cognitive biases can cloud judgment and lead to flawed reasoning, *complacency* may cause you to rely on familiar thinking patterns without questioning their validity. Additionally, the *influence of echo chambers*—environments where only similar viewpoints are shared—can reinforce existing beliefs, thus limiting your exposure to different perspectives. These factors often prevent us from developing a well-rounded perspective.

To overcome these pitfalls, challenge yourself to seek new viewpoints, particularly those that differ from your own, to prevent confirmation bias. Stay engaged with new ideas by reading and staying curious about the world around you. By remaining proactive and intentional in your approach, you can maintain clarity and objectivity in your thought processes, helping you to make better decisions and engage more deeply with the world around you.

How to Improve Your Critical Thinking

Enhancing your critical thinking skills involves regularly sharpening your ability to analyze, evaluate, and reason. This improves your decision-making abilities, aids in solving complex problems, and creates a more thoughtful and deliberate approach to overcoming obstacles.

Socratic Questioning

Socratic questioning is a powerful, albeit rarely discussed, technique for enhancing critical thinking. Named after the ancient Greek philosopher Socrates, this process involves asking a series of thought-provoking questions to explore ideas, uncover underlying assumptions, and stimulate deeper thinking.

At its core, the Socratic method involves the use of questions to guide dialogue and encourage critical examination. Unlike ordinary questions that seek straightforward answers, Socratic questions are designed to provoke reflection, analysis, and discussion. They challenge individuals to think more deeply about their assumptions, reasoning, and the implications of their ideas.

Socratic questioning, used primarily in Law Schools, is not about winning an argument or proving a point. Instead, it's about promoting an open-minded exploration of ideas. By systematically questioning a topic, you can break it down into its fundamental components, examine the validity of the arguments presented, and reveal any inconsistencies or biases in the reasoning.

Here are four fundamental types of Socratic questions:

1. ***Clarification Questions.*** These questions help you better understand the topic by asking for explanations or examples. For example, *"What do you mean by that?"* or *"Can you provide an example?"*

2. ***Probing Assumptions.*** These questions challenge the underlying assumptions behind a statement or argument. For example, *"What assumptions are you making here?"* or *"Is this assumption always true?"*

3. ***Exploring Consequences.*** These questions examine the potential outcomes of an idea or decision. For example, *"What are the implications if this is true?"* or *"What might happen if we take this course of action?"*

4. ***Questioning Viewpoints.*** These questions encourage the examination of different perspectives and the consideration of alternative viewpoints. For example, *"What would someone who disagrees with you say?"* or *"How would this look from another perspective?"*

Using Socratic questioning encourages you to explore topics more thoroughly and to consider multiple perspectives. It also encourages deeper analysis by challenging you to think critically about your assumptions and the logic of your arguments. Additionally, Socratic questioning promotes a more open dialogue where ideas can be examined and debated constructively.

Reflective Thinking

Reflective thinking is another crucial component of critical thinking that involves looking back on your experiences, decisions, and actions to gain deeper insights and improve future performance. By engaging in reflective thinking, you can assess what worked well, what didn't, and why, allowing you to learn from your experiences and make more informed choices in the future. This introspection develops a greater awareness of your thoughts and behaviors, enhancing your overall ability to think critically.

Reflective thinking requires you to pause and consider your experiences and decisions. It's a way to evaluate what you've done, understand your motivations, and identify areas for growth. This allows you to analyze your actions and decisions from a more detached perspective.

By reflecting on past experiences, you can identify patterns in your thinking, recognize biases, and understand how your emotions may have influenced your decisions. This heightened self-awareness is vital to improving your critical thinking skills, as it helps you learn from mistakes, and develop more effective strategies for the future.

Here are some popular techniques for reflection:

- *Journaling.* Writing down your thoughts and experiences is a powerful way to reflect. Journaling allows you to organize your thoughts, express your feelings, and track your progress over time. This gives insights into your behavior and thought patterns, helping you to make more mindful decisions.

- *Meditation.* Meditation encourages mindfulness and self-awareness. By taking a few minutes each day to meditate, you can clear your mind, focus on your thoughts, and reflect on your experiences in a calm, centered state.

- *Structured Self-Assessment.* Using a structured approach to reflection can help you evaluate your decisions more systematically. For example, after completing a project or reaching a milestone, set aside time to assess what went well, what could have been done differently, and what you learned from the experience.

Start by setting aside a specific time each day or week for reflection. This could be as simple as spending a few minutes in the morning or evening to think about your day and consider what you've learned. Use prompts, such as *"What was the most challenging part of my day?"* or *"What could I have done differently?"* to help guide your reflection and make it more focused. Additionally, reviewing past decisions and actions regularly allows you to assess your progress and make adjustments as needed.

When you make reflection a daily practice, you create opportunities for continuous learning and self-improvement. Regular reflection helps you become more aware of your strengths and weaknesses, allowing you to build on your successes and learn from your mistakes. Over time, this habit of introspection leads to better decision-making, increased resilience, and a deeper understanding of yourself and the world around you.

Critical Reading and Writing

Finally, critical reading and writing are powerful skills for developing and demonstrating critical thinking. Expressing your thoughts clearly in writing helps you analyze information, construct logical arguments, and communicate effectively. By honing these skills, you can enhance your ability to think critically and articulate your ideas more persuasively.

Sharpening Critical Reading Skills

Reading critically involves more than just understanding the words on a page; it requires you to actively question its content and evaluate its validity. Critical reading is about digging deep into the material, looking beyond the surface to understand the author's intent, assess the strength of the arguments presented, and identify any underlying biases.

Start by identifying the author's purpose. Ask yourself why the author wrote the piece and what they are trying to convey. Evaluate the evidence presented: *Is it credible? Is it relevant? Does it support the author's claims effectively?* Recognizing biases is also crucial. Consider whether the author has a particular agenda or viewpoint that might skew their interpretation of the facts.

Naturally, different texts require different approaches when it comes to critical reading. For academic papers, focus on the methodology, the quality of the evidence, and the logical coherence of the arguments. With news articles, be aware of potential biases and look for credible sources along with balanced reporting. For opinion pieces, consider the strength of the arguments and the evidence used to support them.

Sharpening Critical Writing Skills

Writing critically is another aspect of developing your critical thinking skills. Critical writing involves constructing clear, logical arguments, supporting your claims with solid evidence, and communicating your ideas in a structured and persuasive manner.

Writing forces you to organize thoughts and articulate your reasoning clearly. It requires you to structure your arguments logically, ensure that each point is supported by evidence, and anticipate potential counterarguments. Through writing, you refine your ideas and improve your ability to communicate complex concepts succinctly and effectively.

Before you begin writing, create a detailed outline that lists your main points and the evidence you'll use to support them. This helps ensure that your argument flows logically and coherently. During drafting, focus on getting your ideas down on paper without worrying about perfection.

Revise the draft carefully, looking for areas where your argument could be strengthened or clarified. Finally, review your work with trusted peers. This can provide valuable insights and help you see your writing from a fresh perspective.

Developing critical reading and writing skills can enhance your ability to engage with information thoughtfully and express your ideas compellingly. These skills are fundamental to effective communication.

In the next chapter, we'll switch gears and begin exploring the concept of deep focus.

Chapter 7

Deep Focus: The Antidote to Distraction

"One machine can do the work of fifty ordinary men. No machine can do the work of one extraordinary man."

— Elbert Hubbard

———◄O►———

I N A WORLD FILLED with endless distractions, the ability to concentrate intensely on a single task is a pivotal skill for long-term success. Sadly, we rarely hear of deep focus or deep work as skills that should be honed, developed, and perfected over time. But know that the greatest innovators of our time all leveraged deep focus and regularly engaged in deep work.

Put simply, deep focus and deep work are your superpowers in a distracted world.

In this chapter, we will explore the role of deep focus as a powerful antidote to the many distractions we face daily. We will examine the benefits of cultivating deep focus, both for enhancing cognitive abilities, career advancement and for improving overall well-being.

Understanding Deep Focus and Deep Work

Deep focus is the ability to immerse yourself fully in a task, blocking out all distractions and engaging with the work at hand. It's not just concentrating—it's about reaching a state of flow where your mind and body are wholly aligned with the activity, leading to heightened productivity and a deeper sense of satisfaction.

What is Deep Focus?

Deep focus is the state of being fully immersed in a task, free from interruptions or distractions. It's about dedicating a significant block of time to work on something that requires intense concentration. Deep focus allows you to engage deeply with the assignment, think critically, and produce high-quality results.

Deep focus is crucial in both personal and professional endeavors. When you can sustain concentration on a single task, you will be more productive, produce higher-quality work, and generate innovative ideas. Deep focus allows you to dive into complex tasks without interruption, leading to more thorough and thoughtful results.

Furthermore, deep focus plays a vital role in mastering complex skills and solving intricate problems. Focusing deeply gives your brain the space to fully process information, make connections, and develop a deeper understanding of the subject matter.

This higher level of engagement is vital for learning new skills, as it enables you to move beyond surface-level knowledge and build expertise over time. Deep focus helps you approach challenges clearly, allowing you to explore various solutions and think critically about the best path forward.

The Link Between Deep Focus and Deep Work

While deep focus is the ability to immerse one's mind fully in a given task, the concept of *"deep work"* refers to the output of that deep focus applied to a specific task. Deep work is a fundamental skill required in technical and high-stakes fields such as software engineering and medicine, where multiple interactions may occur simultaneously.

It's also important to distinguish deep work from shallow work. Deep work is characterized by mentally demanding activities that create significant value. These tasks push your cognitive abilities to their limit and often lead to new insights, learning, or breakthroughs.

In contrast, shallow work consists of tasks that are easy to perform, do not require much thought, and often involve repetitive or logistical activities like checking emails or attending routine meetings. While shallow work may be necessary, it doesn't contribute to the same level of productivity and creativity as deep work.

How the Brain Achieves Focus

Deep focus is not just a mental discipline; it is rooted in complex neurological processes that enable the brain to filter out distractions and sustain attention. This process involves the *prefrontal cortex*, a region of the brain responsible for executive functions such as decision-making, attention control, and goal management. The prefrontal cortex works with other brain areas, like the *parietal lobe*, to maintain focus by suppressing stimuli that could divert attention away from the task at hand.

Neurotransmitters, such as *dopamine* and *norepinephrine*, play a crucial role in sustaining focus. Dopamine, often associated with the brain's reward system, helps reinforce concentration by providing a sense of satisfaction when a task is completed. This reward mechanism supports sustained effort and engagement. Norepinephrine, on the other hand, enhances alertness and attention, particularly during challenging or demanding tasks. These neurotransmitters help create an optimal state for deep focus, allowing you to stay engaged with your work.

The Cognitive Benefits of Deep Focus

Regular deep focus significantly enhances your ability to process information, retain knowledge, and think critically. When you focus intensely on a task, your brain is more efficient at encoding information into memory, which leads to better retention and comprehension. This deep engagement allows you to absorb new material more thoroughly and recall it easily.

Regular deep focus also plays a vital role in enhancing critical thinking. Concentrating deeply gives you the mental space to analyze complex information, recognize patterns, and draw meaningful connections between concepts. This kind of cognitive engagement is essential for developing a deeper understanding of the subject matter and for making well-reasoned decisions.

Moreover, deep focus can have a profound impact on creativity and problem-solving. By maintaining a concentrated state, your brain can better connect seemingly disparate ideas and generate creative solutions. This is because deep focus encourages a more expansive way of thinking, allowing you to explore various possibilities and think *"outside the box."* The ability to sustain attention without interruption creates an environment where creative thoughts can flourish, and innovative ideas can take shape.

Why It's So Hard to Achieve Deep Focus

Undoubtedly, achieving deep focus has become increasingly challenging. Digital distractions and work environments that prioritize constant connectivity over productivity undermine our ability to concentrate deeply on a single task.

The True Cost of Digital Distractions

Digital distractions are among the most potent obstacles to achieving deep focus. Constant notifications, social media alerts, and the temptation to multitask frequently disrupt concentration and block our sustained engagement with a task. Every time a notification pops up, or a new email arrives, it lures our attention away from what we are doing, making it harder to return to the same level of focus. This breaks concentration and diminishes our ability to enter a state of deep work.

The impact of frequent interruptions, often called *"task-switching cost,"* is substantial. When you constantly move from one task to another, your brain needs time to reorient itself and refocus on the new activity.

Research has shown that this cognitive shift can result in lost time and reduced efficiency, as it takes several minutes to regain full concentration after an interruption. The more frequently you switch tasks, the more cognitive resources are spent on reorienting rather than on completing the work at hand, leading to lower overall productivity and higher mental fatigue.

The Decline of Deep Work in the Workplace

Modern work environments further undermine the ability to engage in deep work. Open office spaces, the expectation of constant availability, and the pressure to respond immediately to messages and emails contribute to a culture of constant distraction. While open offices are designed to encourage collaboration and communication, they also lead to frequent interruptions and a lack of privacy, making it difficult to focus on complex tasks that require sustained attention.

Companies generally expect employees to be constantly available and responsive. This expectation naturally leads to an environment where interruptions are frequent and deep work is nearly impossible to achieve. Emails, instant messages, and other forms of communication demand immediate attention, dragging you away from focused tasks and preventing you from reaching a state of deep concentration. Over time, this pattern can undermine your ability to engage in meaningful, uninterrupted work, reducing your overall productivity and job satisfaction.

In most modern cultures, being busy is equated with being productive and successful. This cultural mindset encourages people to fill their schedules with activities and tasks, often at the expense of quality and focus. The glorification of *"busyness"* can create a false sense of accomplishment, where the sheer volume of work is mistaken for genuine, meaningful progress.

This preference for quantity over quality can stifle deep focus, as employees are encouraged to prioritize speed and multitasking over thoughtful, concentrated, high-quality work.

The common misconception that multitasking is synonymous with productivity persists in most professional settings. Multitasking is often perceived as a way to accomplish more in less time, but in reality, it reduces the quality of work and increases the likelihood of errors. When we attempt to juggle multiple tasks simultaneously, our attention is divided, leading to shallow engagement with each activity. This fragmented approach to work prevents the deep focus needed for thoughtful analysis, creative problem-solving, and the completion of high-quality work.

Deep Focus is a Competitive Advantage

As artificial intelligence continues to transform the concept of work, the ability to engage in deep focus quickly becomes a critical differentiator for career advancement. By cultivating deep focus, you can differentiate your value from what AI can deliver and enhance your ability to innovate, lead, and drive significant results in your field.

Deep focus allows humans to excel where AI falls short—creative, strategic, and complex tasks that require sustained attention and intellectual effort. Unlike AI, humans can bring unique perspectives, emotional intelligence, and ethical considerations to their work. By cultivating deep focus, we can explore nuances, generate innovative ideas, and efficient, thoughtful solutions to complex problems.

In industries where AI handles routine tasks, the value of deep work is only growing. As machines take over repetitive functions, the demand for human innovation, problem-solving, and critical analysis only increases. There is a growing need for professionals who can analyze complex data, develop strategies, and create ingenious products in high demand. Deep work enables these individuals to go beyond surface-level solutions and deliver high-impact results.

Deep focus is also a silent contributor to career advancement. Individuals develop deep expertise and knowledge in their chosen fields by mastering the ability to concentrate intensely on specialized tasks. This level of mastery frequently leads to recognition, leadership opportunities, and career growth, as organizations actively seek up-and-coming professionals who think critically and contribute meaningfully to the company's strategic objectives.

The Future of Work: From Routine to Knowledge-Based

As the job market continues to evolve in response to advances in AI and automation, the shift from routine work to knowledge work requires skills that go beyond what machines can do. To remain relevant and competitive, workers must not only excel at their current roles but also continuously learn and adapt to new techniques and methodologies.

The job market is steadily moving toward knowledge-based work that demands higher-order thinking and decision-making. As AI-driven automation takes over mundane duties, the focus naturally shifts to roles that require deep expertise, innovation, and strategic planning.

In this new environment, deep focus becomes essential for knowledge workers. Researchers must immerse themselves in complex studies, developers must concentrate on intricate coding tasks, and executives need uninterrupted time to formulate and execute plans. The practice of deep work allows professionals to devote themselves to the intricacies of their fields, enabling them to contribute more effectively to their organizations' overall goals.

The Role of Deep Focus in Lifelong Learning

Likewise, continuous learning is a necessity in an AI-driven economy. As paradigms and processes evolve rapidly, professionals must constantly update their skills and knowledge to stay current. Deep focus is crucial in this context, as it enables us to absorb new information, practice new skills, and integrate new concepts into our existing knowledge base.

The connection between deep focus and the ability to adapt to new technologies and methodologies is clear: those who focus intensely on learning are better equipped for change and can take advantage of new opportunities. Regardless of the assignment, deep focus allows individuals to continuously learn and apply that knowledge successfully in their work.

By leveraging deep focus as a competitive advantage, we can position ourselves for success in an AI-driven world. This not only supports personal growth and career advancement but also ensures that we remain agile, innovative, and relevant.

Deep Focus and Personal Fulfillment

Beyond professional success, deep focus also plays a significant role in achieving personal fulfillment. By dedicating yourself to meaningful work, you can align your efforts with your values and aspirations, leading to a greater sense of purpose and satisfaction.

Deep focus enables you to stay committed to your long-term personal and professional goals by providing the clarity and discipline needed to make consistent progress. Dedicating time to focused work makes you more likely to overcome challenges, stay motivated, and achieve your goals. This commitment helps you build momentum and resilience, even when faced with setbacks.

Aligning the practice of deep work with your core values and long-term objectives ensures that your efforts contribute to meaningful progress. This provides direction and improves motivation, as you can see the direct impact of your efforts on your personal growth and fulfillment. By focusing on what truly matters, you can achieve greater purpose and satisfaction in your work.

Deep focus also offers numerous psychological benefits, including reduced stress, increased satisfaction, and improved mental health. When you are fully engaged in your work, you are less likely to be distracted by negative thoughts or worries, allowing you to stay present and focused on the task at hand. This immersion can lead to a state of flow, a highly rewarding experience that enhances creativity, productivity, and overall happiness.

In the next chapter, we'll explore practical strategies for cultivating deep focus.

Chapter 8
How to Develop Deep Focus

"The bad news is time flies.
The good news is you're the pilot."
— Michael Altshuler

————◆◇◆————

IN THE LAST CHAPTER, we discussed the science behind deep focus and its importance. In this chapter, we'll explore practical strategies for developing deep focus despite life's constant distractions. You'll learn practical ways to create an environment that supports concentration, develop habits that reinforce focused work, and use mindfulness techniques to enhance attention.

Create a Focus-Friendly Environment

Deep focus requires more than self-discipline and strong willpower; it also requires creating an environment that supports sustained concentration and minimizes distractions. Your surroundings play a crucial role in your ability to maintain deep focus, and by intentionally shaping your environment, you can enhance your capacity for uninterrupted, high-quality work.

A well-designed workspace is essential for achieving deep focus. Your physical environment significantly impacts your ability to concentrate, think clearly, and maintain productivity. By thoughtfully arranging your workspace, you can minimize distractions and create a setting that supports sustained attention.

Minimizing visual and acoustic distractions in your workspace is essential. Start by decluttering your desk and removing unnecessary items that can divert your attention. Keeping your workspace tidy and organized helps create a calm atmosphere, reducing the likelihood of getting sidetracked by irrelevant stimuli. Additionally, consider the placement of your desk and chair—position them in a way that limits exposure to high-traffic areas or windows that may invite interruptions.

A comfortable workspace is equally important for maintaining focus over extended periods. Ergonomics, the study of designing environments that fit the user, plays a key role in this. Invest in a supportive chair that encourages good posture, and ensure your desk is at an appropriate height to prevent strain. Proper ergonomics help prevent physical discomfort and support better concentration by allowing you to focus on your work rather than bodily discomfort.

The Role of Lighting and Sound

Lighting is another vital aspect of your workspace that can significantly affect your ability to concentrate. Natural light is generally the best option for maintaining focus and alertness, as it supports your body's natural circadian rhythms. If natural light isn't available, choose artificial lighting that mimics daylight to help keep you alert and reduce eye strain. Avoid harsh fluorescent lights, which can cause fatigue, and opt for adjustable light — allowing you to customize the brightness to your needs.

Sound is another important factor that can enhance or disrupt your focus. Manage noise levels by using noise-canceling headphones or earplugs to block out background noise that may distract you. Some find that *white noise* or soft background music helps them concentrate by masking more disruptive sounds. For others, a silent environment provides optimal conditions for deep focus, allowing them to fully immerse themselves in work without interruptions.

By carefully designing your workspace with attention to physical layout, ergonomics, lighting, and sound, you can create an environment that helps you perform at your best. A well-thought-out workspace enhances your ability to concentrate, therefore significantly boosting productivity.

Establishing Boundaries to Protect Focus

To sustain deep focus, it's essential to set clear boundaries that protect your concentration from both digital and human distractions. This allows you to work without interruptions, ensuring that your time is spent on meaningful, high-value activities.

Digital devices are generally the most common sources of distraction, with notifications, messages, and alerts constantly vying for attention. To protect your focus, set specific rules for how and when you use these devices.

Turn off non-essential notifications to reduce interruptions, or use *"focus modes"* designed to block distracting websites and apps during work hours. Alternatively, scheduling *"tech-free"* times, such as the first hour of your day or during meals, can also help you maintain focus.

Communicating your boundaries to those around you is also paramount for minimizing interruptions. Initially, it might sound a bit harsh, but others must respect your need for focused time.

Let your colleagues, friends, family, and stakeholders (such as supervisors and managers) know when you need to concentrate and ask them to avoid interrupting you during these periods. Setting clear expectations helps build mutual understanding and consideration for your time and the need to maintain deep focus.

Managing External Distractions

Even with the best intentions, external interruptions are sometimes unavoidable. To manage these disruptions, use techniques that help deflect or minimize their impact. For instance, use a *"do not disturb"* sign or a similar clear indication when engaging in deep work.

Likewise, communicate specific times when you are available for questions and conversations. If someone interrupts you unexpectedly during these restricted times, politely (but firmly) let them know you are in the middle of focused work and arrange a time to reconnect later.

Designing a schedule that supports deep focus also requires planning your day around your energy levels and the nature of your tasks. Block out dedicated periods for deep work, ideally during times when you are most alert and energized. This might be in the morning for some, or later in the afternoon for others.

Conversely, schedule adequate time for shallow work, like answering emails or attending meetings, when your energy might naturally dip. By aligning high-value tasks with your energy levels, you can maximize your productivity throughout the day.

Personal Habits for Deep Focus

Cultivating deep focus also requires developing habits that naturally support sustained attention and concentration. Habits are powerful because they shape our daily routines and determine how we approach life by default. By building habits that reinforce deep focus, you can train your mind over time to concentrate and significantly enhance your ability to full engage with complex tasks.

Build a Routine for Deep Work

A daily routine is one of the most effective ways to promote deep focus. With a set schedule, your brain knows what to expect and can prepare for periods of concentrated effort.

A well-defined routine also reduces decision fatigue by eliminating the need to constantly decide what to do next, allowing you to conserve mental energy for more important tasks. This structured approach enhances productivity by creating a predictable rhythm in your day, making it easier to enter and maintain a state of deep focus.

For some, ***morning rituals*** are a popular choice; starting the day with consistent activities—such as exercise, journaling, or reading—sets a productive tone for the day, thus preparing the mind for deep work.

Time-blocking is another effective strategy, where you allocate specific blocks of time for focused tasks, ensuring you have uninterrupted periods to dive deeply into your work. The *Pomodoro technique*—which involves working for 25 minutes, followed by a 5-minute break—can also help maintain focus and prevent burnout by balancing intense work sessions with brief recovery periods.

Scheduling Deep Work Sessions

To integrate deep work into your routine, schedule specific sessions throughout the day dedicated to focused tasks. Start by identifying your *peak focus times*—that is, the times of day when you are most alert and capable of deep concentration. For many people, this is early in the morning, but it can vary based on individual preferences and energy levels.

Once you've identified these peak times, block them out on your calendar and vigorously protect them from interruptions. Turn off notifications, set your phone to *"Do Not Disturb"* mode, and let colleagues and family members know that you are unavailable during these periods.

Regular deep work sessions are vital to improving your focus and productivity. Consistency helps train your brain to recognize these periods as times for concentrated effort, making it easier to enter a state of deep focus. Consistent deep work also leads to a more structured and predictable workday, which can reduce stress and increase overall work satisfaction.

Maintaining a Focus-Friendly Lifestyle

Once established, deep focus must be a sustained practice to fully reap its long-term benefits. With deep work, you can produce higher-quality results in less time. Concentrated effort on high-value tasks minimizes the inefficiencies of multitasking and frequent interruptions, allowing you to complete work more effectively. This increased productivity helps you meet deadlines and achieve your goals, enabling you to take on more challenging endeavors.

To maximize the benefits of deep focus, it's essential to set clear goals, track your progress, and continuously improve. Start by identifying the most critical tasks that will have the greatest impact on your success and dedicate time for these activities. Use tools like productivity journals or digital trackers to monitor your progress and reflect on your performance.

Self-assessment is a powerful tool for maintaining deep focus. By regularly reflecting on your performance, you can gain insights into your strengths and areas for improvement. This practice helps you stay accountable for reaching your goals, refine your strategies, and make informed decisions about optimizing your focus and productivity.

Sustaining deep focus requires a commitment to continuous improvement and adaptability. Regular reflection on your routines can help you identify what works best for you and where adjustments may be needed. This dedication to continual growth ensures that deep focus remains a core part of your life, contributing to your ongoing success.

In the next chapter, we'll pivot and examine the future of work in the AI era—who wins, who loses, and what this means for society at large.

Chapter 9

The Future of Work: Winners and Losers

"Our technological powers increase, but the side effects and potential hazards also escalate."

— Alvin Toffler

———◆○◆———

T HE RISE OF ARTIFICIAL intelligence is reshaping the global job market at an unprecedented pace. As AI continues to advance, it is creating new opportunities while systematically eliminating others. This change is redefining what it means to be "competitive" in the workforce, with some professions thriving under these changes while others face obsolescence.

In this chapter, we will look at some of the winners and losers of the AI-driven economy. We'll examine a few sectors that are benefiting from AI advancements and others that are being dismantled by automation and machine learning. Additionally, we will discuss skills and how you can position yourself to leverage new opportunities.

The Changing Employment Landscape

The integration of artificial intelligence and automation into the workforce has fundamentally changed how businesses operate and how work is performed. As AI technology continues to advance, it is now a key driver of efficiency, innovation, and cost reduction across virtually every industry.

Here are just a handful of examples. In *manufacturing*, AI-powered robots and automated warehouse management systems are enhancing production lines, optimizing logistics, and reducing downtime. In *finance*, AI algorithms analyze market trends, assess risks, and detect fraudulent activities. The *healthcare* sector is also experiencing significant changes, with AI aiding in diagnostics, personalized medicine, and even robotic surgery, improving patient outcomes and operational efficiency.

The widespread adoption of AI is mainly driven by its ability to allocate human resources to more strategic and creative roles, boosting innovation and competitiveness. The business case for AI adoption is clear: it offers a competitive edge in a rapidly changing market by enabling faster decision-making, minimizing errors, and reducing operational expenses. As AI continues to permeate the economy, understanding its role and impact will be essential for workers and companies to adapt and remain competitive.

"Winners" in the AI-Driven Economy

Artificial intelligence is creating substantial opportunities for those who are prepared to adjust. The AI economy is opening up many new roles, generously rewarding those with the right skills and mindset. These *"winners"* of the AI-driven economy are people who can leverage technology to enhance productivity, innovate, and drive growth.

High-Demand Skills in the AI Era

Not surprisingly, one of the most significant opportunities in the AI economy lies in the growing need for professionals with technical skills and AI development. Expertise in ***data science***, ***machine learning***, and ***software engineering*** has become highly sought after as companies continue to invest in AI technologies to drive innovation and maintain a competitive edge.

Data scientists interpret large datasets to draw meaningful insights and build predictive models. Machine learning engineers develop algorithms that enable machines to learn from data, improving their performance over time without explicit programming. AI software engineers create the frameworks and infrastructure to integrate these advanced technologies into real-world applications.

Undoubtedly, as AI continues to evolve, those who invest in these types of technical skills will be well-positioned to capitalize on the growing opportunities.

While technical skills are crucial, the AI economy also rewards the ability to combine technical knowledge with domain-specific expertise. As AI applications become more integrated into various sectors, professionals who can bridge the gap between AI technology and industry-specific needs are in high demand.

As a result, interdisciplinary roles are emerging, such as *AI ethics specialists* who ensure ethical considerations are integrated into AI development, *AI product managers* who oversee the creation, sale, and distribution of AI-enabled products that meet market needs, and *AI consultants* who advise businesses on how to implement AI solutions effectively.

There will also be a growing need for *AI regulators* and *AI lobbyists* to help "steer" politicians and policymakers toward the responsible use of implementing AI solutions. These roles highlight the growing need for professionals who understand the complex intersection of AI technology and domain expertise, leveraging both to create value.

Non-Technical Roles with High Demand

Before proceeding, it's important to note that not all in-demand fields will require a technical background or specialized AI domain expertise. Fields that require human interaction and specialized skills are extremely difficult for AI (and even advanced robotics) to replicate and cannot easily be replaced. For now, it is simply more cost-effective to keep humans in these roles.

One of the most prominent examples is within the **skilled trades**. College enrollment has skyrocketed over the past few decades, leading to a vast shortage of skilled tradesmen. Fields such as carpentry, plumbing, drywalling, HVAC, elevator installation, and facilities maintenance have been overlooked as merely *"blue-collar"* work, pushing students into (seemingly) lucrative fields requiring college degrees.

However, despite the apparent allure of a college degree, jobs in these non-technical fields often pay more than *"white collar"* jobs requiring college degrees. In fact, many of my close friends in the skilled trades laugh, touting the simple but profound statement: *"I may have dirty hands, but they touch clean money."* Likewise, other high-paying, non-technical fields, including positions with exclusive direct human interaction, such as cosmetology, direct care in nursing homes, mental health professionals, etc., will continue to be in high demand.

The Rise of AI-Augmented Professions

AI is not only creating new job roles but also enhancing traditional professions by augmenting the capabilities of human workers. The concept of AI augmentation involves using AI tools to assist workers, allowing them to perform their jobs more efficiently.

AI augmentation handles routine tasks and provides advanced analytical capabilities. By automating repetitive aspects of a job, AI allows professionals to focus on higher-level tasks that may require human judgment, creativity, and empathy. This collaboration generally enhances productivity, improves decision-making, and leads to better business outcomes.

As AI continues to advance, the trend of human-AI collaboration in the workplace is growing. Rather than replacing all human workers outright, AI is increasingly being used as a co-worker that assists the existing workforce with shared tasks, decision-making, and creative problem-solving. This shift is reshaping the nature of work, creating environments where humans, advanced robotics and AI work closely together.

A growing number of companies are leveraging AI to improve results while retaining human oversight. For instance, in software development, tools like GitHub and CoPilot help developers write code in real-time while AI provides explanations and possible testing scenarios. In customer service, AI chatbots handle routine inquiries, allowing human agents to focus on more complex issues that require empathy and nuanced understanding of product features and limitations.

In manufacturing, AI-powered robots work alongside human workers, performing tasks that require precision and consistency while humans oversee quality control and unstructured problem-solving. Undoubtedly, the future of work will increasingly leverage the strengths of both humans and artificial intelligence to drive efficiency and innovation.

"Losers" in the AI-Driven Economy

While the rise of artificial intelligence presents numerous opportunities, it also brings considerable challenges for many workers and industries. As AI continues to automate tasks and streamline processes, many job roles are increasingly at risk of becoming obsolete. This shift is creating a new job market where some workers find themselves on the losing end of the AI economy, facing job insecurity, stagnant wages, or the need to acquire new skills to remain relevant.

Jobs at Risk of Displacement

As artificial intelligence advances, it will continue to automate tasks traditionally performed by humans. These predictable, repetitive jobs are prime candidates for automation, which can perform these tasks more quickly and accurately and are more cost-effective than human workers.

Some of the job types most vulnerable to AI include:

- **Data Entry.** AI systems can easily handle data entry tasks, processing large volumes of information with low cost, high accuracy, and speed. This reduces the need for human workers, leading to job losses in roles that were once entry points for many workers.

- ***Customer Service.*** Many customer service tasks, especially those that involve answering frequently asked questions or handling simple inquiries, are being automated through chatbots and virtual assistants. These AI-driven tools provide quick responses and can handle multiple interactions simultaneously, significantly reducing the need for human customer service representatives.

- ***Manufacturing Line Work.*** The manufacturing sector has seen significant automation over the years, with AI-powered robots now taking on tasks such as assembly, welding, and quality control. These robots can work continuously without breaks, leading to a reduction in manufacturing jobs.

- ***Administrative Tasks.*** AI is also being used to automate various administrative tasks, such as scheduling, invoicing, and managing emails. These technologies reduce the need for administrative staff, impacting roles that were once seen as stable employment options.

The Impact on Low-Skill and Low-Wage Workers

AI's impact on the job market is not evenly distributed. Low-skill and low-wage workers are disproportionately affected by the rise of automation, as their roles are more likely to involve tasks that can be easily automated.

The challenges of reskilling for displaced workers are significant. Transitioning to new jobs in the AI-driven economy will require new skills. However, reskilling will be a challenge for many displaced workers, particularly those who face barriers such as age, financial constraints, or limited digital literacy.

Furthermore, the pace of technological change means that the demand for specific skills can quickly pivot, making it difficult for low-skill workers to keep up with the shifting requirements of the job market. This creates a cycle of displacement and reskilling that can be challenging for workers to keep up with, especially without adequate support from targeted reskilling programs, social safety nets, and proactive policies that support workers in adapting to the changing job market.

The Paradox of Worker Displacement and Automation Acceleration

As artificial intelligence and automation continue to displace jobs, we will certainly see increased protests, labor movements, and calls for stricter regulation. Workers facing job loss and economic uncertainty will demand better protections, "fair" compensation, and policies that safeguard their livelihoods. However, while these movements attempt to slow down the pace of automation, they will more than likely accelerate it instead.

Mass displacement of workers will lead to increasing social unrest as individuals struggle with the resulting financial instability of unemployment. In response, workers and labor unions will seek to pressure employers and governments to take action. These measures may include increased regulation of AI and automation technologies, higher wages, better working conditions, and more robust social safety nets.

However, these well-intentioned efforts will most likely have the opposite effect. When faced with higher labor costs due to wage demands or stricter regulations that make employing human workers more complex and expensive, companies will be tempted to accelerate their adoption of automation and AI systems as a cost-cutting measure.

Companies fully understand that investing in more advanced automation technologies further reduces their reliance on human labor, thereby avoiding the additional conflict and costs associated with labor disputes and regulatory compliance.

The desire for greater efficiency and productivity will further fuel the push for more complex automation systems. As businesses seek to maintain their competitive edge in a global market already driven by automation, they will turn to more complex AI-driven solutions that can operate 24/7, reduce errors, and optimize operations without the challenges associated with managing a human workforce.

This creates an interesting paradox where efforts to protect jobs through protests and regulations will, in all likelihood, lead to faster adoption of technologies that displace even more workers. This paradox underscores the dilemma between the short-term needs of workers and the long-term implications of technological advancement.

"Hollowing Out" the Middle Class

The displacement of jobs due to artificial intelligence and automation is not just a challenge for individual workers; it also has far-reaching societal implications. As AI reshapes the job market, it has the potential to create unprecedented economic inequalities, leading to significant shifts in how wealth and opportunities are distributed.

One of the most pressing concerns about AI displacement is the increase in economic inequality. As AI systems automate low-skill jobs, the gap between high-skill and low-skill workers will likely widen.

This trend will continue to *"hollow out"* the middle class, as many mid-skill jobs that traditionally provide stable employment and upward mobility are lost. Jobs that have historically been accessible to a broad range of workers with moderate levels of education and training are among those most susceptible to automation.

As these jobs disappear, the pathways to social mobility become narrower, making it harder for workers to transition into higher-paying, more secure positions. This *"hollowing out"* effect could lead to a polarized job market, with a small number of high-skill, high-wage positions and a larger number of low-skill, low-wage positions but fewer opportunities in between.

As the gap between the wealthy and poor widens, increased social unrest and demands for policies such as stronger social safety nets and increased taxation will no doubt increase.

The Psychological Impact of AI-Driven Job Loss

These shifts will also profoundly affect the psychological well-being of the workforce. As AI displaces jobs, many individuals will face not just economic uncertainty but also intense emotional and mental despair.

Job loss can have severe psychological effects on individuals, as work often provides more than just financial stability. It is a source of identity, purpose, and social interaction. When workers are displaced, the sudden loss of these elements can lead to significant mental and emotional distress.

Not surprisingly, losing a job generally triggers feelings of stress, anxiety, and depression. The uncertainty of finding new employment, coupled with financial strain, can be overwhelming. Moreover, the perception that one's skills are no longer valuable in the evolving job market can lead to a loss of self-esteem and confidence.

Long-term unemployment or underemployment can also result in a range of severe mental health challenges, including chronic stress, clinical depression, and anxiety disorders. The persistent struggle to secure stable employment can erode a person's sense of worth and purpose, leading to feelings of hopelessness and social isolation.

Free or low-cost access to mental health support will be critical for individuals dealing with the emotional toll of job displacement. Therapy, counseling, and support groups will be in high demand to help individuals process their emotions, manage stress, and develop coping mechanisms.

Adapting to the AI Job Market

Adapting to the changes and challenges presented by AI is essential for workers and businesses of all sizes. Thriving in this new environment requires a proactive approach, where employees and organizations must be willing to learn, adapt, and innovate.

The Importance of Lifelong Learning

As job markets rapidly evolve, the ability and willingness to continuously learn and adapt is more critical than ever. The skills required to succeed will constantly change as AI technologies advance and reshape industries. Therefore, a commitment to lifelong learning is vital for those who want to remain competitive and relevant in their careers.

This means that the skills in demand today may not be as valuable tomorrow. As technology evolves, it requires us to constantly update our knowledge and skills. This need for continuous skill development is a hallmark of the AI-driven economy, where adaptability and flexibility are essential to long-term success.

To stay ahead of the curve, as forward-thinking individuals, we must commit to ongoing education and skill investment. Traditional education paths, while still valuable, are just not enough in this type of dynamic environment. *Online learning platforms*, *boot camps*, and *micro-credentials* are vital resources to gain new skills and adapt to market demands quickly.

Let's look at a few of these in more detail:

- *Online Learning Platforms.* Websites like Coursera, Udemy, and edX offer a variety of courses in emerging fields. These platforms provide flexible yet affordable learning options that fit into any schedule, helping busy professionals to learn new skills at their own pace without committing to long-term education programs.

- *Boot Camps.* Coding boot camps and intensive training programs are designed to quickly teach specific skills, such as programming, cybersecurity, or data analysis, in much less time than a traditional 4-year degree program. These boot camps are typically short-term, focused, and hands-on, providing practical experience that can immediately be applied in the workplace.

- *Micro-Credentials.* Micro-credentials and digital badges offer another way to gain recognition for specific skills or competencies. These credentials are often granted after completing a course or passing an assessment, allowing a person to showcase their expertise in a particular area. Micro-credentials are particularly valuable in the AI-driven job market, where employers seek candidates with specialized skills that can be verified quickly and easily.

By taking advantage of these learning opportunities, individuals can continuously develop skills, stay current with industry trends, and position themselves for success in the AI economy.

Embracing a Growth Mindset

In addition to continuous learning, thriving in the AI economy requires a psychological shift towards a *growth mindset*. Coined by psychologist Carol Dweck, a growth mindset is the belief that abilities and intelligence can be developed through dedication and hard work. This perspective contrasts with a fixed mindset, where individuals believe their talents and intelligence are static traits.

Embracing a growth mindset is crucial in a world where in-demand skills are constantly in flux. Viewing challenges as opportunities for growth rather than as threats allows you to remain open to new experiences, learn from failures, and adapt to new circumstances. In the AI era, where the need to learn and evolve is paramount, a growth mindset supports resilience.

Here are some techniques for cultivating a growth mindset:

- *Continuous Learning:* Commit to lifelong learning by regularly seeking out new knowledge and skills. Stay curious and motivated to learn, whether through formal education, self-study, or hands-on experience. Embrace the idea that learning is a continuous process, and there is always something new to discover.

- *Adaptability:* Be willing to adapt to new situations and challenges. In a rapidly changing economy, flexibility is essential. Stay open to change, be prepared to pivot quickly if necessary, and view adaptation as an opportunity to grow and thrive.

- *Resilience:* Develop resilience by learning to bounce back from setbacks and failures. Understand that failure is a natural part of the learning process and an opportunity to gain valuable insights. Use these experiences to improve, grow stronger, and build confidence in your ability to overcome obstacles.

By focusing on continuous skill development and cultivating a growth mindset, you can better navigate the challenges and opportunities of the AI-driven job market. These qualities will enable you to remain competitive, resilient, and ready to embrace the future of work.

In the next chapter, we'll discuss the controversial topic of Universal Basic Income (UBI) in the AI-driven economy.

Chapter 10

UBI In the Age of AI

"We should measure welfare's success by how many people leave welfare, not by how many are added."
— Ronald Reagan

A S ARTIFICIAL INTELLIGENCE CONTINUES to transform industries and, therefore displace jobs, the idea of Universal Basic Income (or, UBI) has steadily gained traction as a viable solution to many of the economic challenges posed by automation. UBI represents a radical shift in how society supports individuals in an economy experiencing widening disparities.

In this chapter, we will examine the concept of Universal Basic Income (UBI) in the AI era. We will discuss the arguments for and against UBI, its potential impact on economic inequality, and how it could reshape the relationship between work and financial security.

The Concept of Universal Basic Income (UBI)

Universal Basic Income (UBI) is a policy proposal that suggests providing a regular, unconditional sum of money to every individual, regardless of their employment status or income level. The ultimate goal of UBI is to ensure a basic level of financial security for all, helping to mitigate some of the economic disparities caused by technological advancements.

The seriousness and urgency of UBI discussions are centered around the difficult question: *"If automation and AI displace a large enough segment of the working population, who buys the stuff that the robots produce?"*

The fundamental principles of UBI are:

- *Universality.* Every individual receives the same payment, ensuring that the policy is inclusive and applies to all citizens equally.

- *Unconditionality.* There are no restrictions or prerequisites for receiving the income, allowing recipients to spend it as they see fit without government oversight or obligation.

- *Regularity.* Payments are made consistently, such as monthly or annually, providing a basic, predictable, and stable source of income for all.

These underlying principles distinguish UBI from traditional welfare programs, which generally target specific populations or require individuals to meet certain eligibility criteria.

The concept of UBI is not new and has its roots in various philosophical and economic ideas proposed throughout history. Early discussions of UBI can be traced back to thinkers like Thomas More, who imagined a society without poverty in his work *"Utopia,"*[1] who suggested a basic endowment for all citizens as a fundamental right.

Over time, UBI has evolved from a Utopian idea into a topic of serious political and economic debate. In the 20th century, the concept gained traction among economists and policymakers as a potential solution to poverty and inequality. More recently, the rise of automation and AI has brought renewed attention to UBI as a way to address the economic disruptions caused by technological advancements.

The Economic and Social Justifications for UBI

UBI is often touted as a viable solution to increasing job displacement caused by automation. One of the main arguments for UBI is its potential to reduce economic inequality by providing a financial safety net for all citizens. By ensuring that

---

1. See, e.g., The World Forum on Peace and Security, *"Universal Basic Income: The Future of Civilization?"* Retrieved from https://www.psforum.org/u niversal-basic-income-the-future-of-civilization/

everyone has access to a basic income, proponents of UBI claim it will lift people out of poverty and provide a safety net for those affected by technological change

Pilot programs in countries like Finland and Canada have shown that UBI can reduce financial stress and improve overall well-being. These studies suggest that providing a guaranteed income can help individuals meet their basic needs, reduce reliance on other forms of social assistance, and improve quality of life. However, despite its potential benefits, UBI remains a controversial and hotly debated topic, with strong arguments both for and against its implementation.

Arguments in Favor of UBI

Those in favor of UBI argue that it offers several economic and social benefits:

- *Economic Benefits.* UBI could stimulate economic demand by increasing individuals' purchasing power, possibly boosting economic growth. It could also reduce poverty by providing a guaranteed income floor, ensuring everyone has access to basic resources. Furthermore, UBI could simplify the financial and administrative overhead of current welfare systems by replacing multiple targeted programs with a single, universal payment.

- *Social Benefits.* Beyond economic considerations,

UBI could improve social outcomes by reducing stress and anxiety associated with financial insecurity. By providing a stable income, UBI could improve health, prevent social collapse, and allow people to pursue education, creative endeavors, or volunteer work without the constant pressure of financial survival.

Criticisms and Concerns

On the other hand, critics of UBI raise several concerns about its feasibility and potential downsides:

- *Cost.* One of the primary criticisms of UBI is the cost of implementing such a program on a large scale. Critics argue that the financial burden of providing a basic income to all citizens is unsustainable and requires substantial tax increases or cuts to other social services. Additionally, concerns about the potential impact of inflation, dollar destabilization, and work incentives persist—with some fearing that a guaranteed income may eliminate the motivation for being productive members of society.

- *Social Concerns.* Some critics also worry that UBI could further create dependency, undermine work ethic, and lead to an overall decline in productivity. There are also concerns that UBI will not adequately address the root causes of poverty and inequality, such as lack of access to quality education and healthcare.

As the debate around UBI continues, it is essential to weigh these arguments carefully and consider the broader implications of implementing such a policy.

Potential UBI Implementation Models

Various models for implementing UBI are being proposed to address the economic challenges of an AI-driven world. Each model offers different approaches to balancing the ideals of universality and equity with practical considerations such as cost and political feasibility.

Fully Universal UBI

A *fully universal UBI* is a model in which all citizens receive the same amount of income from the government, regardless of their employment status, income level, or any other criteria. This approach is based on the principle of universality and aims to provide a basic level of financial security for everyone.

Under this model, every individual would receive a regular, unconditional payment from the government. The payment would be designed to cover basic living expenses, ensuring that all citizens can access essential resources such as food, shelter, and healthcare. The universality of this model eliminates the need for means-testing or eligibility criteria, simplifying the distribution process and ensuring that no one is excluded.

The Potential Benefits and Drawbacks of a Universal Approach:

- **Benefits.** One of the primary benefits is its simplicity. By providing the same amount to everyone, the government can avoid the administrative complexities and costs associated with determining eligibility and managing multiple welfare programs at State and Federal levels. This simplicity also ensures that all citizens, regardless of circumstances, have access to a basic income.

- **Drawbacks.** However, the universal approach also has its drawbacks, particularly in terms of cost. Providing a UBI to all citizens, regardless of their financial need, would require an incredible source of government funding, which would most likely lead to higher taxes or cuts to other public services. Critics also argue that a fully universal UBI is not the most equitable approach, as it provides the same benefit to wealthy individuals, diverting resources away from those who need them most.

Targeted or Conditional UBI

An alternative to a fully universal UBI is a ***targeted or conditional UBI***. This model focuses on providing financial support to specific groups of people or making payments conditional on meeting certain criteria, such as income level or participation in training programs.

In a targeted UBI model, payments are directed toward people believed to be most in need, such as low-income families or unemployed workers. On the other hand, Conditional UBI might require recipients to engage in certain activities, like reskilling or community service, to qualify for the income.

How Targeting Could Make UBI More Affordable and Politically Feasible:

- *Affordability.* Targeted or conditional UBI models can significantly reduce the overall cost of the program by limiting payments to specific groups or setting conditions for eligibility. This makes UBI more fiscally sustainable, as it concentrates resources on those most likely to benefit from the support rather than providing payments to all citizens regardless of need.

- *Political Feasibility.* Targeted or conditional UBI models may also be more politically acceptable, as they can address concerns about fairness and resource allocation. Such models can garner broader support from policymakers and the public by ensuring that public funds are used efficiently and directed toward those most affected by economic disruptions. Additionally, linking UBI to activities like training programs can help ensure that recipients are actively working to improve their skills and employability, addressing concerns about long-term dependency and work incentives.

The future of UBI could take various forms, ranging from fully universal models to more targeted or conditional approaches. Each model presents unique benefits and challenges, and the implementation choice will depend on society's needs, values, and resources at any given time.

UBI and the Future of Work

The concept of Universal Basic Income (UBI) has far-reaching implications for the future of work. By providing a guaranteed income to all, UBI could fundamentally change how we think about employment and economic participation by providing a financial foundation that enables more flexible and non-traditional work arrangements.

UBI supporters argue that one of the most significant potential benefits of UBI is its ability to promote entrepreneurship. By providing a basic level of financial security, UBI could reduce the financial risks associated with starting a business or pursuing an innovative idea. Aspiring entrepreneurs will then be free to invest time and resources into developing their ventures without the fear of financial ruin if their efforts do not succeed. This could lead to increased innovation, new business creation, and economic growth as more individuals are empowered to take entrepreneurial risks.

However, as critics of UBI point out, this argument seems weak and circuitous because it ignores the basic premise behind the underlying need for UBI. If there are truly no jobs (and limited opportunities) remaining from automation and AI (necessitating the need for UBI), how will entrepreneurship opportunities create new work *en masse*?

UBI vs. Social Instability

Beyond its economic impact, supporters of UBI argue that it could significantly influence social cohesion by reshaping how individuals relate to each other and to society as a whole. However, the more likely scenario is that UBI, at best, would prevent social and societal collapse.

By providing a guaranteed income to all citizens, UBI could help reduce some economic anxiety and promote a sense of **equality and security**. When individuals are less worried about meeting their basic needs, they may be more likely to engage positively with their communities. UBI could also promote a sense of shared purpose, reinforcing the idea that everyone deserves a basic level of security and dignity.

However, the unspoken concern is, "*What happens if AI and automation continue to displace large portions of the workforce and UBI is not implemented?*" The consequences are almost too frightening to think about. People will find ways to survive, regardless of whether the law sanctions it.

At best, UBI would provide a backstop for complete societal collapse and anarchy. Even with social welfare problems in place, violent crime has continued to become an epidemic. Moreover, countries like Venezuela and Haiti paint a grim picture of what life might look like without basic economic protections for citizens.

My Personal Thoughts on UBI

I believe that UBI has great potential to be beneficial if and when automation and AI remove large swaths of the vulnerable population from the workforce. However, there is even greater potential for misuse and waste. We only need to look back at the COVID-era pandemic stimulus efforts to see how people *really* react when given money for no work, along with the economic repercussions.

The pandemic stimulus efforts represented the largest non-wartime government spending initiative in history. Nearly 6 Trillion dollars were printed in the span of 3 years, causing massive inflation that we are still reeling from today as I sit down to write this book in late 2024.

Additionally, reports of widespread fraud and abuse of the now infamous PPP (Paycheck Protection Program) continue to surface in news headlines. Can we honestly say that the economy, overall, is in better shape because of the stimulus efforts? Are the after-effects of massive inflation worth it? Given the constant headlines of people complaining that they can't afford basic necessities, including food, transportation, housing, and healthcare, the stimulus payments that were once so welcome now seem to be a distant memory.

Notwithstanding the fact that the U.S. dollar is supported only by credit and goodwill, the question is, *"Who ultimately pays the bill for UBI?"* Arguments that the rich should "pay their fair share" ignore the reality that, overall, the wealthy are taxed disproportionately higher than everyone else. They also generally tend to be the largest segment of employers.

Now, this is not to ignore the harsh consequences of wealth inequality, but income tends to follow assets, and assets tend to be the result of value creation. There will always be value inequality (i.e., some citizens will always produce more value than others), so in a capitalist system, there will always be some level of income inequality.

Today, there are more social welfare programs than at any other time in history. Yet, underlying societal problems persist. While we like to think that society's ills are rooted in a lack of money, I believe they are rooted in something much deeper—a lack of purpose, and an overwhelming sense of entitlement. No amount of UBI will cure these evils.

Moving On . . .

Looking to the future, whether UBI becomes a widely adopted policy will depend on many factors, including current trends, political will, and public support. The conversation around UBI has gained momentum in recent years, fueled by the increasing awareness of AI's impact on employment. Pilot programs around the world have shown both promise and challenges, offering insights into how such a system might work in practice.

However, for UBI to become mainstream, significant obstacles must be overcome. Securing funding, navigating political opposition, and designing a system that effectively meets the needs of a diverse population are all substantial challenges. Despite these hurdles, the growing interest in UBI suggests that the idea is not going away. As technology continues to reshape our lives, the need for innovative solutions will only become more pressing.

It's important to recognize that UBI is not a one-size-fits-all solution. There are significant risks and challenges associated with its implementation, including its potential impact on work incentives and social stability. As we consider UBI's role in the future, we must remain mindful of these complexities.

Let's conclude our journey together with some final thoughts.

Chapter 11

Final Thoughts

*"Adapt or perish, now as ever,
is nature's inexorable imperative."*

— H. G. Wells

A S ARTIFICIAL INTELLIGENCE AND automation redefine the skills needed for success, it's clear that critical thinking and deep focus are essential. In a world where machines handle routine tasks, our ability to engage in complex problem-solving, think creatively and concentrate deeply sets us apart.

Adapting to an AI-Driven Future

As new roles emerge and traditional jobs are displaced, the need for critical thinking, deep focus, lifelong learning, and adaptability becomes paramount. Staying relevant and competitive in an AI-driven world requires a commitment to continuous self-driven education and the flexibility to adapt to new challenges and opportunities.

Adopting a growth mindset is crucial for thriving in the AI era. This mindset encourages us to view challenges not as obstacles but as opportunities for learning and development. By being open to change and willing to adapt, we can use AI advancements as catalysts for personal and professional growth. Resilience becomes vital in navigating this rapidly changing world; it's about embracing uncertainty and using it as a stepping stone towards greater achievement.

Final Reflections

As we conclude our journey, it's essential to reflect on how we can best navigate the challenges and opportunities that lie ahead. The AI era presents unprecedented changes but also offers significant potential for growth, innovation, and progress. By embracing a mindset that values adaptability and resilience and prioritizing human values alongside technological advancement, we can ensure that we will thrive in this ever-evolving landscape.

While AI and automation offer numerous benefits, it's equally important to weigh these advancements against the preservation of fundamental human values. Creativity, empathy, and ethical responsibility are qualities that technology cannot replicate, and they should guide our approach to integrating AI into our lives.

We must ensure that technological progress serves humanity's best interests, enhancing our quality of life without compromising the core values that define us as human beings.

The future of AI has the potential to revolutionize industries, create new forms of employment, and change the way we live and work. However, with these advancements come unforeseen challenges and risks requiring careful consideration and proactive management. The evolving relationship between humans and machines will shape the future of society, influencing everything from our daily lives to global economies.

The journey towards an AI-driven world requires action. Continuous self-improvement is vital—stay informed, remain curious, and actively seek new opportunities for growth. By taking deliberate steps to enhance your skills and knowledge, you position yourself to better navigate the complexities of the AI era.

Now is the time to implement the strategies in this book. Stay consistent and gradually build towards larger goals. Remember, the journey is just as important as the destination. Regularly reflect on your progress, assess how these practices are influencing your personal and professional growth, and make adjustments as needed. Your path is unique—embrace it with intention and purpose.

Remember, the choices you make today will shape the world of tomorrow. Stay inspired, continue learning, and let your journey continue to be one of growth, innovation, and meaningful contributions.

With Love and Gratitude,

Donovan Garett

www.ingramcontent.com/pod-product-compliance
Lightning Source LLC
Chambersburg PA
CBHW032004190326
41520CB00007B/351